D0449945
Jr. Chemhead
Written & Illustrated
by B. K. Hixson
EMULSIFIERS, SUSPENSIONS, OXIDIZERS ?
OK YOUR TURN.
YEP. YEP. NOPE.

First Printing • October 2001
B. K. H-ixson

Published by Loose in the Lab, Inc.
9462 South 560 West
Sandy, Utah 84070

www.looseinthelab.com

Library of Congress Cataloging-in-Publication Data:

Hixson, B. K.
Jr. Chemhead/B. K. Hixson
p. cm.-(Loose in the Lab Science Series)

Includes index
ISBN 0-9660965-9-2
1. Chemistry experiments-juvenile literature. [1. Chemistry experiments 2. Experiments] I. B. K. Hixson II. Loose in the Lab III. Title IV. Series
QP441.D54 2001
152.14

Printed in the United States of America
All hail to Mendeleyev!

Dedication

Aubrey Dee Hixson

(The Junior Chemhead in the Hixson Lab)

I am sure you would have preferred to have been anointed "Princess" rather than "Chemhead," but as your Grandma used to tell me, "If you are going to complain, you should have been more selective when you were picking out your parents." Besides, when you get older, making the transition to "Parrothead" will be effortless.

Here's to years of exploring the world together. There are no goals unattainable, no sphere of knowledge beyond your grasp. I love mooshing your fat cheeks and rocking you to sleep in my arms these days but look forward to the explosion of ideas, art, music, and conversation that I am certain you brought with you to share. What a ride it will be.

Hugs & Kisses,

♡Dad

Acknowledgments

Getting a book out for public consumption is far from a one-man job. There are lots of thank-yous to be doodled out and at the risk of leaving someone out, we attempt to do that on this page. In terms of my chemistry education, at the top of the list is Mr. Ed Goffard, my fifth -grade teacher at Shaver Elementary School in Portland, Oregon. He introduced us to the world of crystals, solutions, precipitation reactions, and all of the wonderful treasures that could spring forth from a beaker if the right concoction was mixed—my first taste of chemistry. Next I would like to thank whomever wrote the *Anarchist's Cookbook* and simultaneously apologize to anyone who was either accidentally or intentionally a participant in one of the reactions suggested in that book.

As for my educational outlook, the hands-on perspective, and the use of humor in the classroom, Dr. Fox, my senior professor at Oregon State University, gets the credit for shaping my educational philosophy while simultaneously recognizing that even at the collegiate level we were on to something a little different. He did his very best to encourage, nurture, and support me while I was getting basketloads of opposition for being willing to swim upstream. There were also several colleagues who helped to channel my enthusiasm during those early, formative years of teaching: Dick Bishop, Dick Hinton, Dee Strange, Connie Ridgway, and Linda Zimmermann. Thanks for your patience, friendship, and support.

Next up are all the folks that get to do the dirty work that make the final publication look so polished but very rarely get the credit they deserve. Our resident graphics guru Ben Francom gets a nod for scanning and cleaning the artwork you find on these pages, as well as putting together the graphics that make up the cover. A warm Yankee yahoo to Sue Moore our editor who passes her comments on so that Kathleen Hixson, Diane Burns, and Sue Moore (once again) can take turns simultaneously proofreading the text while mocking my writing skills.

Once we have a finished product, it has to be printed by the good folks at Advanced Graphics—Michael Williams, Matt and the crew—so that Stefan Kohler, Louisa Walker, and the Delta Education gang can market and ship the books, collect the money, and send us a couple of nickels. It's a short thank-you for a couple of very important jobs.

Mom and Dad, as always, get the end credits. Thanks for the education, encouragement, and love. And for Kathy and the kids—Porter, Shelby, Courtney, and Aubrey—hugs and kisses.

Repro Rights

There is very little about this book that is truly formal, but at the insistence of our wise and esteemed counsel, let us declare: *No part of this book may be reproduced or utilized in any form or by any means, electronic or mechanical, including photocopying, recording, or by any information storage and retrieval system, without permission in writing from the publisher.* That would be us.

More Legal Stuff

Official disclaimer for you aspiring scientists and lab groupies. This is a hands-on science book. By the very intent of the design, you will be directed to use common, nontoxic, household items in a safe and responsible manner to avoid injury to yourself and others who are present while you are pursuing your quest for knowledge and enlightenment in the world of chemistry. Just make sure that you have a fire blanket handy and a wall-mounted video camera to corroborate your story.

If, for some reason, perhaps even beyond your own control, you have an affinity for disaster, we wish you well. *But we, in no way take any responsibility for any injury that is incurred to any person using the information provided in this book or for any damage to personal property or effects that are directly or indirectly a result of the suggested activities contained herein.* Translation: You're on your own, despite the fact that many have preceded you in the lab. Take heed from our friend Johnny, who was a chemist, but is a chemist no more. For what he thought was H_2O was H_2SO_4.

Less Formal Legal Stuff

If you happen to be a home schooler or very enthusiastic school teacher please feel free to make copies of this book for your classroom or personal family use—one copy per student, up to 35 students. If you would like to use an experiment from this book for a presentation to your faculty or school district, we would be happy to oblige. Just give us a whistle and we will send you a release for the particular lab activity you wish to use. Please contact us at the address below. Thanks.

Special Requests
Loose in the Lab, Inc.
9462 South 560 West
Sandy, Utah 84070

Table of Contents

Dedication	3
Acknowledgments	4
Reproduction Rights	5
Who Are You? And. . . How to Use This Book	10
Lab Safety	16
Recommended Materials Suppliers	19

The National Content Standards (Grades K–4)

1. Objects have many observable properties, including size, weight, shape, color, temperature, and the ability to react with other substances. Those properties can be measured using tools, such as rulers, balances, and thermometers.

2. Objects are made of one or more materials, such as paper, wood, and metal. Objects can be described by the properties of the materials from which they are made, and those properties can be used to separate or sort a group of objects or materials.

3. Materials can exist in different states—solid, liquid, and gas. Some common materials, such as water, can be changed from one state to another by heating or cooling.

The National Content Standards (Grades 5-8)

These standards are listed in our other chemistry book, Le Boom du Jour, which covers more advanced topics than this book.

The 10 Big Ideas About Chemistry & Corresponding Labs

1. Matter is any living or nonliving thing that takes up space. No two chunks of matter can occupy the same space at the same time.

Lab #1: Pouring Air (Gas/Liquid)	*22*
Lab #2: Paper Clip Stew (Solid/Liquid)	*25*
Lab #3: Effervescence (Solid/Gas)	*28*
Lab #4: Density Column (Liquid/Liquid)	*32*
Lab #5: Eggzasperating Puzzle (Solid/Liquid)	*37*
Lab #6: Dancing Bubbles (Gas/Gas)	*41*

2. Objects have many observable properties, including size, weight, shape, color, temperature, and the ability to react with other substances. Those properties can be measured using tools, such as rulers, balances, and thermometers.

Lab #7: Thermometer Rules! 46
Lab #8: Cubit Catastrophe 50
Lab #9: Beakers, Flasks, & Graduated Cylinders 54
Lab #10: Double Pan Weigh In 57
Lab #11: Bird Bonz 60

3. Matter can exist in three different states: solid, liquid, or gas. Matter changes state when the temperature goes up or down. The point of change, independent of the volume of the sample, is predictable and is recorded as the freezing and as the boiling points.

Lab #12: Cubes to Clouds (Melting/Boiling/Condensing) 64
Lab #13: Swiss Cheese Candles (Melting/Freezing) 70
Lab #14: See-Thru Fat (Melting/Freezing) 73
Lab #15: The Ice-Cube Roundup (Freezing) 76

4. The smallest unit of matter is called an atom. There are roughly 100 different kinds of atoms. These tiny building blocks, also called elements, are organized from smallest to largest in a chart called the Periodic Table of the Elements. This table describes very specific characteristics about each element that allows scientists to identify them.

Lab #16: Chem Shorthand 80
Lab #17: Iron Inquiry (Magnetism) 84
Lab #18: Sulfur Bombs (Smell) 86
Lab #19: Sorting Sugar & Salt (Shape) 88
Lab #20: Decomposing Carbon (Color) 90
Lab #21: BS Fire Extinguisher (State) 92

Even More Contents

5. Elements can combine or bond with one another in groups of two or more forming molecules. When this happens, a new compound is formed that has its own, unique set of characteristics.

Lab #22: Marshmallow Molecules 97
Lab #23: Baking-Soda Cannon (State) 100
Lab #24: Steel Wool Sparkler (Oxidation) 102
Lab #25: Envious Pennies (Reduction) 104
Lab #26: Mrs. Stewart's BBQ Garden (Crystallization) 107

6. A physical change is different from a chemical change and can be identified when matter goes through a change in shape, size, or state.

Lab #27: Simply Physical (Size & Shape) 111
Lab #28: Eco Peanut Puzzle (State) 114

7. A solution is a mixture of different kinds of matter made up of solvents (liquid) and solutes (molecule-sized solids) that are mixed together evenly. Other kinds of mixtures are emulsions, suspensions, and colloids.

Lab #29: Mixing Oil and Water (Emulsion) 119
Lab #30: Mutant Milk Maggots (Suspension) 122
Lab #31: Elmer's Bouncing Blob (Colloid) 125

8. Once new compounds form, the elements tend to remain connected together. Mixtures, on the other hand, are made up of different kinds of matter that can be separated from one another using filters, crystallization, evaporation, or even magnets.

Lab #32: Muddy Waters (Filtration) 130
Lab #33: Snowstorm in a Tube (Precipitation) 131
Lab #34: Ironing Out Sand (Magnetism) 134
Lab #35: Salt Crust Pan (Evaporation) 137
Lab #36: Creepy Colors (Chromatography) 139

9. Solids, liquids, and gases can diffuse into liquids and gases. The rate they diffuse is affected by temperature, pressure, and concentration.

Lab #37: Slow-Motion Rainbow (Concentation) 143
Lab #38: Thermal Ink Clouds (Temperature) 146
Lab #39: Mixing Colors Race (Concentration) 149
Lab #40: Dehydrated Grape Dance (Pressure) 152

10. Water is a bipolar molecule. This arrangement of two positively charged hydrogen atoms and one negatively charged oxygen atom produces a weak electromagnetic attraction that is responsible for the phenomena of surface tension, capillary action, and cohesion.

Lab #41: Water Slide 156
Lab #42: Centering a Cork 158
Lab #43: Obedient Bubbles 161
Lab #44: One-Way Cheesecloth 164
Lab #45: Paper Boat Race 167
Lab #46: Scared Pepper 170
Lab #47: Exploding Oil Drops 173
Lab #48: Jumping Paper 176
Lab #49: Giant Bubble Machine 179
Lab #50: The Instant Bubbler 183

Science Fair Projects
A Step-by-Step Guide: From Idea to Presentation 186
Step #1: The Hypothesis 194
Step #2: Gather Information 203
Step #3: Design Your Experiment 208
Step #4: Conduct the Experiment 213
Step #5: Collect and Display Data 215
Step #6: Present Your Ideas 219

Glossary 223
Index 229

Who Are You ? And ...

First of all, we may have an emergency at hand and we'll both want to cut to the chase and get the patient into the cardiac unit if necessary. So, before we go too much further, **define yourself**. Please check one and only one choice listed below and then immediately follow the directions that follow *in italics*. Thank you in advance for your cooperation.

I am holding this book because. . .

___ **A. I am a responsible, but panicked, parent.** My son/daughter/triplets (circle one) just informed me that his/her/their science fair project is due tomorrow. This is the only therapy I could afford on such short notice. Which means that if I was not holding this book, my hands would be encircling the soon-to-be-worm-bait's neck.

Directions: Can't say this is the first or the last time we heard that one. Hang in there, we can do this.

1. Quickly read the Table of Contents with the worm bait. The Big Ideas define what each section is about. Obviously, the kid is not passionate about science, or you would not be in this situation. See if you can find an idea that causes some portion of an eyelid or facial muscle to twitch.

If that does not work, we recommend narrowing the list to the following labs because they are fast, use materials that can be acquired with limited notice, and the intrinsic level of interest is generally quite high.

Lab 4 • Density Column • page 32
Lab 11 • Bird Bonz • page 60
Lab 14 • See-Thru Fat • page 73
Lab 30 • Mutant Milk Maggots • page 122
Lab 36 • Creepy Colors • page 139
Lab 42 • Centering a Cork • page 158
Lab 48 • Jumping Paper • page 176

How to Use This Book

2. Take the materials list from the lab write-up and from page 209 of the Science Fair Project section and go shopping.

3. Assemble the materials and perform the lab at least once. Gather as much data as you can.

4. Go to page 186 and read the material. Then start on Step 1 of Preparing Your Science Fair Project. With any luck you can dodge an academic disaster.

___ **B. I am worm bait.** My science fair project is due tomorrow, and there is not anything moldy in the fridge. I need a big Band-Aid™, in a hurry.

Directions: Same as Option A. You can decide if and when you want to clue your folks in on your current dilemma.

___ **C. I am the parent of a student who informed me that he/she has been assigned a science fair project due in six to eight weeks.** My son/daughter has expressed an interest in science books with humorous illustrations that attempt to explain chemistry and associated phenomena.

Who Are You? And ...

Directions: Well, you came to the right place. Give your kid these directions and stand back.

1. The first step is to read through the Table of Contents and see if anything grabs your interest. Read through several experiments, see if the science teacher has any of the more difficult materials to acquire like diffraction gratings, polarizing filters, and some of the chemicals, and ask if they can be borrowed. Play with the experiments and see which one really tickles your fancy.

2. After you have found and conducted an experiment that you like, take a peek at the Science Fair Ideas and see if you would like to investigate one of those or create an idea of your own. The guidelines for those are listed in the Science Fair section. You have plenty of time so you can fiddle and fool with the original experiment and its derivations several times. Work until you have an original question you want to answer and then start the process. You are well on your way to an excellent grade.

___ **D. I am a responsible student and have been assigned a science fair project due in six to eight weeks.** I am interested in chemistry, and despite demonstrating maturity and wisdom well beyond the scope of my peers, I too still have a sense of humor. Enlighten and entertain me.

Directions: Cool. Being teachers, we have heard reports of this kind of thing happening but usually in an obscure and hard-to-locate town several states removed. Nonetheless, congratulations.

Same as Option C. You have plenty of time and should be able to score very well. We'll keep our eyes peeled when the Nobel Prizes are announced in a couple of decades.

How to Use This Book

___ **E. I am a parent who home schools my child/children.** We are always on the lookout for quality curriculum materials that are not only educationally sound but also kid- and teacher-friendly. I am not particularly strong in science, but I realize it is a very important topic. How is this book going to help me out?

Directions: In a lot of ways we created this book specifically for home schoolers.

1. We have taken the National Content Standards, the guidelines that are used by all public and private schools nationwide to establish their curriculum base, and listed them in the Table of Contents. You now know where you stand with respect to the national standards.

2. We then break these standards down and list the major ideas that you should want your kid to know. We call these the Big Ideas. Some people call them objectives, others call them curriculum standards, educational benchmarks, or assessment norms. Same apple, different name. The bottom line is that when your child is done studying this unit on chemistry you want them not only to understand and explain each of the ten Big Ideas listed in this book, but also, to be able to defend and argue their position based on experiential evidence that they have collected.

3. Building on the Big Ideas, we have collected and rewritten 50 hands-on science labs. Each one has been specifically selected so that it supports the Big Idea that it is correlated to. This is critical. As the kids do the science experiment, they see, smell, touch, and hear the experiment. They will store that information in several places in their brains. When it comes time to comprehend the Big Idea, the concrete hands-on experiences provide the foundation for building the Idea, which is quite often abstract. Kids who merely read about density gradients, physical vs. chemical changes, and bipolar molecules, or who see pictures of emulsions, suspensions, and colloids but have never squeezed them between their fingers are trying to build abstract ideas on abstract ideas and quite often miss the mark.

Who Are You ? And ...

For example: I can show you a recipe in a book for chocolate chip cookies and ask you to reiterate it. Or I can turn you loose in a kitchen, have you mix the ingredients, grease the pan, plop the dough on the cookie sheet, slide everything into the oven, and wait impatiently until they pop out eight minutes later. Chances are that the description given by the person who actually made the cookies is going to be much clearer because it is based on their true understanding of the process, ***because it is based on experience.***

4. Once you have completed the experiment, there are a number of extension ideas under the Science Fair Extensions that allow you to spend as much or as little time on the ideas as you deem necessary.

5. A word about humor. Science is not usually known for being funny even though Bill Nye, The Science Guy, *Beaker from* Sesame Street, *and* Beakman's World *do their best to mingle the two. That's all fine and dandy, but we want you to know that we incorporate humor because it is scientifically (and educationally) sound to do so. Plus it's really at the root of our personalities. Here's what we know:*

When we laugh ...

a. Our pupils dilate, increasing the amount of light entering the eye.

b. Our heart rate increases, which pumps more blood to the brain.

c. Oxygen-rich blood to the brain means the brain is able to collect, process, and store more information. Big I.E.: increased comprehension.

d. Laughter relaxes muscles, which can be involuntarily tense if a student is uncomfortable or fearful of an academic topic.

e. Laughter stimulates the immune system, which will ultimately translate into overall health and fewer kids who say they are sick of science.

f. Socially, it provides an acceptable pause in the academic routine, which then gives the student time to regroup and prepare to address some of the more difficult ideas with a renewed spirit. They can study longer and focus on ideas more efficiently.

g. Laughter releases chemicals in the brain that are associated with pleasure and joy.

6. If you follow the book in the order it is written, you will be able to build ideas and concepts in a logical and sequential pattern. But that is by no means necessary. For a complete set of guidelines on our ideas on how to teach home-schooled kids science, check out our book, Why's the Cat on Fire? How to Excel at Teaching Science to Your Home-Schooled Kids.

How to Use This Book

___ F. **I am a public/private school teacher,** and this looks like an interesting book to add ideas to my classroom lesson plans.

Directions: It is, and please feel free to do so. However, while this is a great classroom resource for kids, may we also recommend several other titles: What's It Matter? *(Basic Intro to Chemistry),* The Labware Jungle *(Learning to ID and use Labware),* Snot In a Box, *(Polymers & Colloids),* A pH Primer *(Acids, Bases, & pH),* and Soup, Goop and Other Poop *(Mixtures, Emulsions, & Solutions),* and That's the Point *(Solids, Liquids, Gas).*

These books have teacher-preparation pages, student-response sheets or lab pages, lesson plans, bulletin board ideas, discovery center ideas, vocabulary sheets, unit pretests, unit exams, lab practical exams, and student grading sheets. Basically everything you need if you are a science nincompoop, and a couple of cool ideas if you are a seasoned veteran with an established curriculum. All of the ideas that are covered in this one book are covered much more thoroughly in the other two. They were specifically written for teachers.

___ G. **My son/daughter/grandson/niece/father-in-law** is interested in science, and this looks like fun.

Directions: Congratulations on your selection. Add a gift certificate to the local science supply store and a package of hot chocolate mix and you have the perfect rainy Saturday afternoon gig.

___ H. **My cooking class is concerned about the decomposition of fatty acids in a high pH environment, in particular, with respect to the role of bonding sites relative to temperature sensitivity. Can you help?**

Directions: Nope. Try the Sous Chef down the street.

Lab Safety

Contained herein are 50 science activities to help you better understand the nature and characteristics of chemicals as we currently understand these things. However, since you are on your own in this journey we thought it prudent to share some basic wisdom and experience in the safety department.

Read the Instructions

An interesting concept, especially if you are a teenager. Take a minute before you jump in and get going to read all of the instructions as well as warnings. If you do not understand something, stop and ask an adult for help.

Clean Up All Messes

Keep your lab area clean. It will make it easier to put everything away at the end and may also prevent contamination and the subsequent germination of a species of mutant tomato bug larva. You will also find that chemicals perform with more predictability if they are not poisoned with foreign molecules.

Organize

Translation: Put it back where you get it. If you need any more clarification, there is an opening at the landfill for you.

Dispose of Poisons Properly

This will not be much of a problem with the labs that are suggested in this book. However, if you happen to wander over into one of the many disciplines that incorporates the use of more advanced chemicals, then we would suggest that you use great caution with the materials and definitely dispose of any and all poisons properly.

Practice Good Fire Safety

If there is a fire in the room, notify an adult immediately. If an adult is not in the room and the fire is manageable, smother the outbreak with a fire blanket or use a fire extinguisher. When the fire is contained, immediately send someone to find an adult. If, for any reason, you happen to catch on fire, **REMEMBER: Stop, Drop, and Roll.** Never run; it adds oxygen to the fire, making it burn faster, and it also scares the bat guano out of the neighbors when they see the neighbor kids running down the block doing an imitation of a campfire marshmallow without the stick.

Protect Your Skin

It is a good idea to always wear protective gloves whenever you are working with chemicals. Again, this particular book does not suggest or incorporate hazardous chemicals in its lab activities. This is because we are primarily incorporating only safe, manageable kinds of chemicals for these labs. If you do happen to spill a chemical on your skin, notify an adult immediately and then flush the area with water for 15 minutes. It's unlikely, but if irritation develops, have your parents or another responsible adult look at it. If it appears to be of concern, contact a physician. Take any information that you have about the chemical with you.

Lab Safety

Save Your Nose Hairs

Sounds like a cause celebre L.A. style, but it is really good advice. To smell a chemical to identify it, hold the open container six to ten inches down and away from your nose. Make a clockwise circular motion with your hand over the opening of the container, "wafting" some of the fumes toward your nose. This will allow you to safely smell some of the fumes without exposing youself to a large dose of anything noxious. This technique may help prevent a nosebleed or your lungs from accidentally getting burned by chemicals.

Wear Goggles If Appropriate

If the lab asks you to heat or mix chemicals, be sure to wear protective eyewear. Also have an eyewash station or running water available. You never know when something is going to splatter, splash, or react unexpectedly. It is better to look like a nerd and be prepared than schedule a trip down to pick out a Seeing Eye™ dog. If you do happen to accidentally get chemicals in your eye, flush the area for 15 minutes. If any irritation or pain develops, immediately go see a doctor.

Lose the Comedy Routine

You should have plenty of time scheduled during your day to mess around, but science lab is not one of them. Horseplay breaks glassware, spills chemicals, and creates unnecessary messes— things that parents do not appreciate. Trust us on this one.

No Eating

Do not eat while performing a lab. Putting your food in the lab area contaminates your food and the experiment. This makes for bad science and worse indigestion. Avoid poisoning yourself and goobering up your lab ware by observing this rule.

Happy and safe experimenting!

Recommended Materials Suppliers

For every lesson in this book we offer a list of materials. Many of these are very easy to acquire, and if you do not have them in your home already, you will be able to find them at the local grocery or hardware store. For more difficult items we have selected, for your convenience, a small but respectable list of suppliers who will meet your needs in a timely and economical manner. Call for a catalog or quote on the item that you are looking for, and they will be happy to give you a hand.

Loose in the Lab
9462 South 560 West
Sandy, Utah 84070
Phone 1-888-403-1189
Fax 1-801-568-9586
www.looseinthelab.com

Delta Education
80 NW Boulevard
Nashua, NH 03601
Phone 1-800-442-5444
Fax 1-800-282-9560
www.delta-ed.com

Nasco
901 Jonesville Ave.
Fort Atkinson, Wisconsin 53538
Phone 1-414-563-2446
Fax 1-920-563-8296
www.nascofa.com

Ward's Scientific
5100 W Henrietta Road
Rochester, New York 14692
Phone 800-387-7822
Fax 1-716-334-6174
www.wardsci.com

Educational Innovations
151 River Road
Cos Cob, Conneticut 06807
Phone 1-888-912-7474
Fax 1-203-629-2739
www.teachersource.com

Frey Scientific
100 Paragon Parkway
Mansfield, Ohio 44903
Phone 1-800-225-FREY
Fax 1-419-589-1546
www.freyscientific.com

Fisher Scientific
485 S. Frontage Rd.
Burr Ridge, Il 60521
Phone 800-955-1177
Fax 1-800-955-0740
www.fisheredu.com

Flinn Scientific
PO Box 219
Batavia, Il. 60510
Phone 1-800 452-1261
Fax 1-630-879-6962
www.flinnsci.com

The Ideas, Lab Activities, & Science Fair Extensions

Big Idea 1

Matter is any living or nonliving thing that takes up space. No two chunks of matter can occupy the same space at the same time.

Pouring Air

The Experiment

To start exploring this idea that no two things can occupy the same space we are going to experiment with two very common kinds of matter, air and water.

A glass full of air is going to be submerged upside down into a tank of water. This traps the air inside the glass. A second glass is submerged right side up and fills with water as you dunk it into the tank. Without taking either glass out of the water, you are going to be able to "pour" the air underwater from one glass to the other. And for an encore, pour it back again. To further this idea of no two things occupying the same space you are then going to use air from your lungs to empty a glass full of water while it is completely submerged in water.

Materials

1 Aquarium, sink, or large tub
2 12 oz. clear, drinking cup
Water, 5 to 10 gallons
1 Pair of Lungs
1 Straw, bendable

Procedure

1. Fill the large container—either sink, aquarium, or tub—full of warm water. We prefer aquariums from a spectator's point of view.

2. Dunk one glass into the water and let it fill up with water. Take another cup and push it into the water upside down so it traps a cup full of air underwater.

3. Holding the cup full of water upside down above the cup full of water, gently tip the cup full of air to the side, allowing bubbles to escape upward into the cup directly above it. Observe what happens as you continue to empty the cup of air into the cup of water. Describe what you see in the space provided in the Data & Observations section.

4. Now reverse the process, and the cups, and pour the air back into the cup that it came from. Observe what happens to the air inside the cup.

5. Another way to fill the cup full of air is to hold a bendable straw under the water and blow bubbles so that they rise up and are trapped inside the cup.

Data & Observations

1. Describe what happens to the water in the cup as the air is poured into it. ____

____.

2. Describe what happens to the water in the cup as the air is blown into it. ____

____.

Pouring Air

How Come, Huh?

The inverted drinking glass trapped the air inside when it was shoved under the water. However, air is less dense than water and if it is free to move it will be pushed to the surface by the more dense water molecules. So when you tip the glass, the air molecules appear to rise toward the second cup, but in reality, the heavier water molecules are sliding around the bubble of air and pushing it upward. As the air bubbles enter the cup, they are trapped by the plastic or glass again and they start to displace or push water out of the cup so they have room to hang out. No two globs of matter, no matter how small or large, can occupy the same physical space.

The same kind of thing happens with the straw. Your lungs force the air down the straw, but the second it leaves the opening of the straw it starts to expand and is pushed upward by the surrounding water molecules, until it is trapped by the other cup where it displaces the water once again.

Science Fair Extensions

1. Demonstrate that this experiment would work if you varied the temperature of the water.

2. Figure out a way to demonstrate this same idea with two liquids. Find two liquids with different densities, like water and cooking oil, and set up an experiment.

3. Would this experiment work if you placed a very small hole in the bottom of the first, clear, plastic cup that was holding the air? How about the second plastic cup that was full of water? What would happen if both plastic cups had small holes in the bottom?

Paper Clip Stew

The Experiment

The Toobe is our name for a tall acrylic cylinder with a snap-on base that we have designed and manufacture to help teach chemistry and other science topics to kids. None of the experiments in this book requires that you go out and buy a Toobe, we just reference it for convenience. We will always suggest a substitute item.

Start with your Toobe, or a drinking glass, completely full of water. We define "completely full" as the water level being exactly even with the top of the container. Figure out a way to add 50 paper clips to the Toobe without spilling any water.

There are two constraints: One, physically removing any of the water by spilling, drinking, or using an absorbent material like a towel or baby diaper is a blatant violation of the creative process. And two, your time limit for completing this activity once you have received inspiration is a mere 10 minutes; so if you were planning on waiting for the water to evaporate, keep thinking—you just hit a dead end.

Materials

1 Toobe or large drinking glass
1 Box of paper clips
Water

Data & Observations

It is a bit odd, but we are going to ask you to make a prediction before you start the lab. Look at the size of the paper clip, compare that with the size of the container and make an educated guess:

I predict that I will be able to add ____ paper clips to my Toobe before it spills.

I was actually able to add ____ paper clips to my Toobe before it spilled.

Paper Clip Stew

Procedure

1. Fill your Toobe so that the water is perfectly level across the very top of it. Predict how many paper clips you will be able to add and record that number in the space provided on the previous page.

2. Start adding and counting paper clips. Don't stop until you either add 50 or finally add one too many and the water in your Toobe spills over on to the table. Record the number of paper clips that you added to achieve this glorious feat in the space on the previous page.

3. If you get to 50, the water has not spilled, and you want to keep going, please do. You may be surprised at the number of paper clips that you can actually get into the Toobe before you flood the table.

How Come, Huh?

Every time you add a paper clip to the Toobe, the paper clip sinks to the bottom of your container. As it does this, it pushes up a tiny little bit of water exactly equal to its volume. After a couple of paper clips, you would normally think that this would cause a very full container to spill some of the liquid out of the Toobe and on to the table. But because water molecules are attracted to each other—a phenomenon called cohesion, they hang on to their buddies if it looks like one of them might fall over the edge.

The reason they hang on to one another is explored extensively in the last section of this book, but we will touch on it here. If you could see a water molecule it would look like Mickey Mouse's head. The oxygen atom has a negative charge, and the two hydrogen atoms have a positive charge. The result is a molecule that acts like a magnet.

As more and more paper clips are added to the Toobe, more and more water molecules are shoved up out of the container and appear to be balancing above the rim. What is actually happening is the water molecules are attracted to one another and are not easily pulled apart. Because they are not easily intimidated in response to being displaced they form a bulge—visual evidence of surface tension.

This goes on for a while, the bulge growing with every paper clip that is added. Eventually gravity takes its toll on the water molecules, they cannot hang on to one another any longer, and some of them dribble over the edge. But if you watch carefully, they go as a group, hanging on to one another all the way down to the table top.

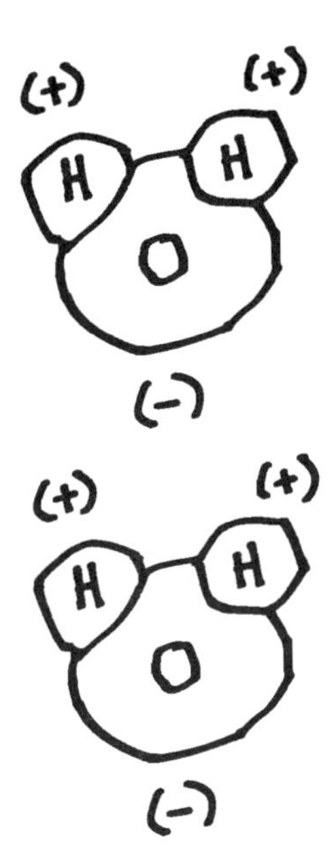

Science Fair Extensions

4. Repeat the experiment with several other items—pennies, brads, bolts, nuts—and see if the result is the same or if this is just peculiar to paper clips. In fact, while you are at it, try adding more water to the container and see if you can create the bulge that way.

5. Try this same experiment with different solutions. Not all liquid molecules are attracted to one another. Make a list of 10 common liquids and decide which ones have surface tension and which ones do not.

6. Design an experiment that explores whether or not temperature has any effect on the surface tension of water.

Effervescence

The Experiment

Effervescence is the term that is used when a gas is forced out of solution. But we had better back up a couple of steps and find out how the gas got into that solution in the first place.

When the good folks who produce soda pop are about ready to bottle their fine, nutritious product, they force molecules of gas, called carbon dioxide, into the spaces between the molecules of the liquid. The way that they do this is to use a lot of pressure. The gas is shoved into the liquid, the bottle is capped while the gas and liquid are still under pressure, and the finished product is shipped to the store. When you buy the bottle of pop and you remove the cap, you also release the pressure trapped inside. The gas escapes, and the soda pop starts to fizz.

You can accelerate the release of the gas from solution by adding salt. Since no two different pieces of matter can occupy the same space the salt shoves the gas out of the way. Effervescence!

Materials

1 Toobe or 12 oz. drinking cup
1 5" pie tin
1 Can of soda pop, 12 oz.
Napkins (optional)
1 Packet of sodium chloride
1 Packet of sugar

Procedure

1. Place the Toobe in the pie tin. This will hopefully catch most of the mess, but just in case, have the napkins handy.

2. Fill the Toobe with 6 ounces of the soda pop of your choice. Examine the soda, look at the bubbles that are escaping from the solution, and draw a picture of what you see. Record your observations in the first box in the Data & Observations section on the next page.

3. After you have completed your observations, quickly add the entire packet of sodium chloride (table salt) to the soda pop, and observe what happens. Examine the Toobe and draw a picture of what you see. Record your observations in the second box in the Data & Observations section.

4. Rinse the Toobe and the pie tin out, and add the remaining 6 oz. of soda pop to the newly cleaned Toobe. Place the Toobe back in the pie tin. Instead of salt, you are going to add sugar this time. Examine the Toobe and draw a picture of what you see. Record your observations in the third box in the Data & Observations section.

Effervescence

Data & Observations

How Come, Huh?

The gas that is trapped in soda pop is called carbon dioxide. It is the same gas that we breathe out of our lungs. It is also matter; and matter, as you know, takes up space. When you fill your lungs with air, your chest expands because you are filling it with matter. When you exhale, the matter leaves your lungs, and your chest occupies less space.

Salt is also matter, and according to people who know about these things, two chunks of matter *cannot* occupy or share the same space. Something gets shoved out of the way. The same thing happens when you sit in a bathtub. The water (matter) in the bathtub gets pushed out of the way by you (more matter). You and the water cannot share the same space.

When the salt was added to the soda pop, the salt shoved the gas out of the way and took its place—because two chunks of matter cannot share the same space. As the gas floated to the top, it surrounded itself with a little bit of the soda-pop liquid; and when it got to the surface it formed a colloid—a gas dispersed in a liquid that we also call a foam. "OK, that's great, but what about the effervescence thing?" you ask. Effervescence is a term that is used to describe when a gas is replaced or shoved out of the way by another substance.

Science Fair Extensions

7. Repeat the experiment, but try it with a can of soda pop that has been open for 24 hours. In addition to leaving the soda open and exposed to the air for that long, pour it back and forth several times to accelerate the removal of the carbon dioxide.

8. Instead of salt try different kinds of sugar. Compare granulated sugar with powdered sugar, with cane sugar, and with liquid sugar water. Does the size of the granules have any effect? Does the sugar have any effect at all? At least your soda won't taste bad once you're done with the experiment.

9. Next time you get to take a ride on the Space Shuttle or your friendly aliens decide to kidnap you a second time, would it be possible to perform this experiment in space? Just another thought. Locate a vacuum pump and chamber. Place a glass full of soda in the vacuum chamber and reduce the air pressure to zero. Try to determine what would happen if you then had a way to add salt.

Density Column

The Experiment

Density is a word that describes how tightly packed the atoms inside a material are. For example, if you were to take two rocks—pumice and granite, you would find that they are made out of exactly the same mix of minerals. They are identical, except that the granite was formed when a big blob of molten rock cooled very slowly underground, and the pumice was formed when the exact same molten mass of rock was spit out of a volcano. If you placed both rocks in water, the granite would sink and the pumice float. The granite is more dense than—packed tighter together than—the pumice.

Another way to explore this idea is using liquids. All liquids have different densities. If you could shrink down to the size of an atom, you could swim around inside a glass of water and then in a glass of corn syrup, and you could compare which one was more crowded. Chances are the corn syrup would win that contest. The lab you are about to do will allow you compare the different densities of five liquids.

Materials

1 Toobe or 500 ml graduated cylinder
1 100 ml graduated beaker or cylinder
5 5 oz. Wax cups
50 ml Water
50 ml Rubbing alcohol
50 ml Glycerin
50 ml Corn syrup

50 ml Vegetable oil
1 Bottle of blue food coloring
1 Bottle of green food coloring
1 Bottle of red food coloring
3 Craft sticks
1 Pen
1 Roll of masking tape

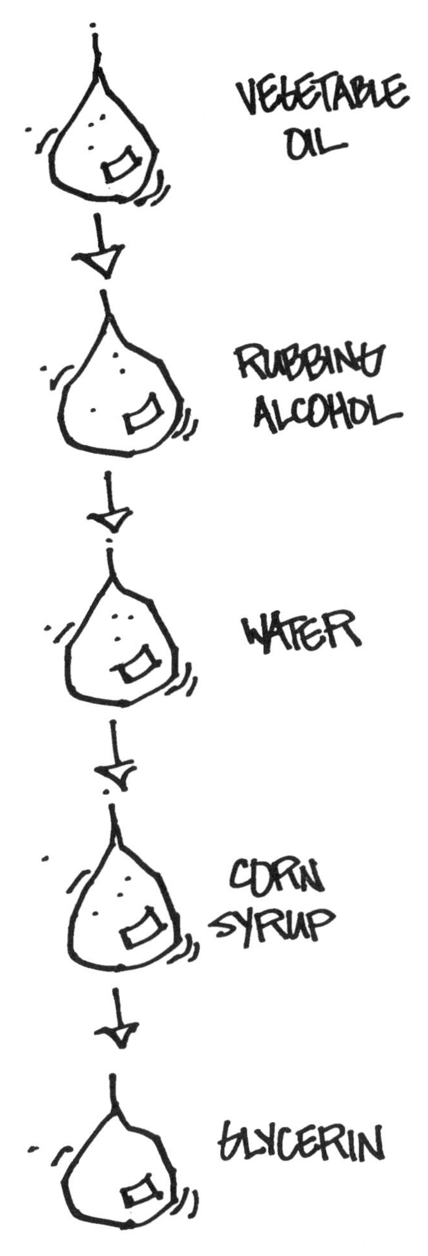

Procedure

1. Add 50 ml of water to wax cup one and label it: Cup 1 - Water. Add 50 ml of the four remaining liquids to four cups and label them respectively: Cup 2 - Rubbing Alcohol, Cup 3 - Glycerin, Cup 4 - Corn Syrup, and Cup 5 - Vegetable Oil.

2. Add the following food colors to the respective liquids: Cup 1 - Water - blue food coloring, Cup 2- Rubbing Alcohol - green food coloring, and Cup 3 - Glycerin - red food coloring. Using craft sticks mix the food coloring into the liquids until they are uniform.

3. Using your fingers, eyes, and any other instruments that you were born with, touch, look at, examine, and compare the five liquids. Order them from thickest (most dense) to thinnest (least dense) and record your predictions in the spaces provided on the next page.

Density Column

4. Based on your observations and prediction add the thickest liquid to the bottom of the Toobe. Then tilt the Toobe at a 45-degree angle and SLOWLY add what you believe to be the next thickest liquid. If this liquid is less dense than the first liquid, it will remain on top of the first liquid. If it is heavier, it will displace the liquid and sink under it.

5. Add the remaining liquids in a similar fashion, following the order that you predicted. When you have added the fifth and last liquid, record your findings in the Data & Observations section. For each liquid that you predicted correctly, place a check mark in the space provided.

6. Now comes the fun part. Place your hand over the open end of the Toobe and shake the liquids up and down, mixing them together. Some of the liquids are very similar in their densities and will mix. Let it sit for a day, then observe how they settle out. Compare the order of the pre-mixed Toobe with the Toobe that you sloshed all over the place.

Data & Observations

Predict the order of density for the five liquids in this experiment. Use your senses to determine that order.

Thickest	Cup #	Liquid
1		
2		
3		
4		
5		

Record your findings after you have actually stacked the liquids into the Toobe.

Thickest	Cup #	Liquid
1		
2		
3		
4		
5		

How Come, Huh?

As we mentioned in the opening, density is a term that describes how tightly packed together a material is. In the case of the glycerin and corn syrup you have long, heavy chains of hundreds of atoms floating very close to one another in solution. When you compare that to water, which has a measly three atoms, it is no wonder that the water is less dense than the glycerin.

Science Fair Extensions

10. Make your own density column using liquids of your choice. If you have access to a double pan balance, you can weigh identical volumes of liquids and make very accurate predictions of which liquids will float in which position in the Toobe.

Density Column

11. Locate a source for dry ice. Try the grocery store or look under "Ice" in the Yellow Pages™. Dry ice is solid carbon dioxide and sublimates from a solid to a gas without becoming a liquid. It is also very nasty stuff. If given the chance to come in contact with skin, it will kill cells almost immediately. **Have an adult help you with this material.**

If you place the dry ice in an aquarium, in a large plastic tub, or in a sink that has been plugged, it will fill the tub with a gas that is heavier, or more dense, than air.

To prove this, blow soap bubbles over the tub and allow them to float down into the container. When the bubbles—full of air from your lungs—come in contact with the carbon dioxide, they stop falling and will rest directly on the layer of heavier, more dense gas. Cool. Try rocking the container (unless it is a sink) and you will see the bubbles rolling back and forth as the heavy gas sloshes around inside the container.

12. Create an experiment that allows solid objects to sort by density when they are shaken in a Toobe.

Eggzasperating Puzzle

The Experiment

Three containers, three clear liquids, three eggs—all we need now are the Three Stooges, but alas, they have all retired to the Big Lab in the Sky so we'll have to wing it.

Like the previous lab, this lab also addresses density. You are going to take three identical containers, fill them with three liquids, and place a fresh egg in each container. Despite apparent similarities in these conditions, the egg in the first container sinks right to the bottom. The egg in the second container is not interested in sinking at all, and instead, floats right on top of the liquid. The third egg, truly an individual, decides to neither sink or float but simply hover in the middle? Density weirdness is alive and well.

Materials

3 Eggs, fresh
3 Toobes, or 12 oz. drinking glasses
1 Pound of salt
1 Spoon
Water

Eggzasperating Puzzle

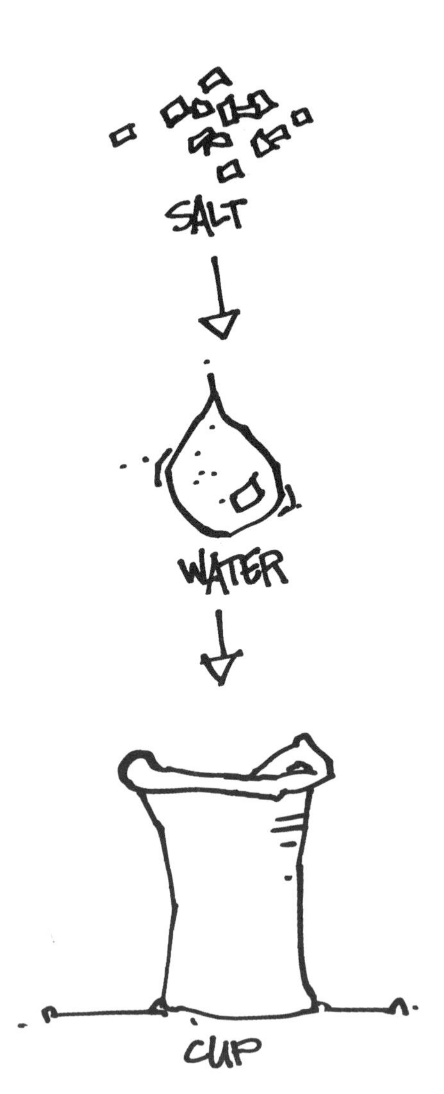

Procedure

1. Fill Toobe or drinking glass number 1 full of water. That's it, not too glamorous.

2. Fill Toobe number 2 half full of water and add four heaping spoons of salt. Hold your hand over the open end of the Toobe and shake the container until all of the salt dissolves or until your arms get tired.

Fill the container full of water and continue to shake, dissolving the remaining salt. If you use warm water, you will find that the dissolving of the salt goes a little faster.

3. Fill Toobe number 3 half full of water and add four heaping spoons of salt. Once again, hold your hand over the open end of the Toobe and shake the container until all of the salt dissolves.

Place the spoon inside the glass or Toobe and slowly pour water into the container on top of the layer of salt water. As the water level rises, lift the spoon up also to minimize the mixing of the fresh water with the salt water. Fill the container all the way to the top.

4. Finally, add an egg to each container. The best way to do this is to place the egg in the spoon and lower the spoon into the liquid, rolling the egg out of the spoon gently.

Data & Observations

In the spaces provided below draw the location of each egg after you placed it in the container. Identify the liquid contents of each container on the lines placed below the boxes.

How Come, Huh?

All liquids produce what is called a buoyant force. It is the force of the molecules in the liquid that push up on a foreign body that is in the liquid. When you added salt to the water, you increased the buoyant force of the liquid.

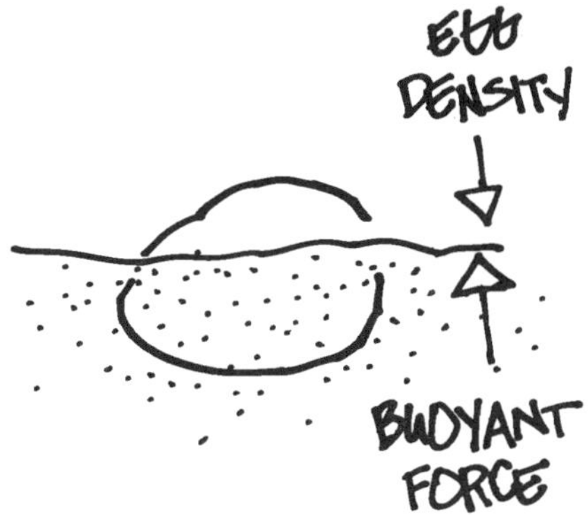

Eggzasperating Puzzle

Here's what happened in each case. Toobe number 1 contained fresh water. The weight of the egg was greater than the buoyant force of the water so the egg sank. In Toobe number 2, the salt increased the buoyant force of the water significantly, so much so that the weight of the egg was supported by the liquid. Toobe number 3 is your sneaker. The weight of the egg was too great for the buoyant force of the fresh water in the top half of the Toobe. When the egg sank far enough to encounter the salt water layer, it stopped sinking because the buoyant force at that point in the solution was great enough to support it.

Science Fair Extensions

13. You can repeat the experiment and get a little more sophisticated by incorporating additional containers. Vary the ratios of the salt water to fresh water. Set the lab up before your friends come over to see it, and you can have five different containers with eggs floating all the way from the top to the bottom and four different places in-between. Drives 'em crazy.

14. Place two different cans of soda pop in a tub of water. One can is regular soda pop and the other, diet. One will float, one will sink, answers please. Experiment with different brands of soda and diet soda pop. Try regular cola, root beer, lemon lime, and the diet versions of the same drink. Graph your results.

Dancing Bubbles

The Experiment

Here's another density experiment that also demonstrates that different kinds of matter cannot occupy the same space.

Here we go: Soap bubbles are blown into the air over an aquarium. They snake some hang time, but eventually gravity gets the best of the situation and the bubbles are pulled down into the aquarium full of dry ice. The funny thing is that they do not sink to the bottom of the aquarium, but instead, they mysteriously float and bounce in the middle of the tank, supported by a gas that is much denser than air. Your task, should you assume the responsibility for this investigation, is to determine why the bubbles did not sink to the bottom of the container—and where did the gas come from in the first place?

Materials

1 Pair of gloves, rubber
1 Pair of goggles (optional)
1 Pound of dry ice (Adult supervision needed)
1 Cloth or paper bag
1 Hammer
1 10 gallon aquarium or plugged up sink
1 Bottle of bubble solution with wand
1 1 gallon plastic bucket

Dancing Bubbles

Procedure

1. *Dry ice is 109 degrees Fahrenheit below zero. If you touch it with bare hands, you run the risk of freezing the skin cells solid, which tends to kill them instantly. Be safe and use the gloves. You will avoid a lot of pain and the unsightly appearance of greenish-black fingers.*

With the help of an adult who has gloved hands set the dry ice on a hard surface. Cover it with a cloth or insert it in a paper bag, and smash it into little pieces with the hammer. Again, with gloved hands, either empty the pieces of dry ice directly from the bag into the aquarium or remove the cover, pick up the dry ice pieces, and place them in the aquarium.

2. Allow the dry ice pieces to stand undisturbed in the bottom of the aquarium for a couple of minutes. Dry ice is the solid form of carbon dioxide. At room temperature, dry ice undergoes a process called *sublimation*, changing directly from a solid to a gas. As you wait, the aquarium will fill up with this invisible carbon dioxide gas. Because carbon dioxide is heavier than air, it displaces, or pushes the air up and out of the aquarium.

3. After two or three minutes, take the bubble solution and blow bubbles *over* the top of the aquarium so that they float down into it. Do not blow down into the aquarium or you will blow the gas out of the container. Observe the bubbles. This is where they get weird. The carbon dioxide in the tank is heavier than the air trapped in the bubbles, so they look like spheres bobbing up and down on an invisible ocean of gas—which, curiously enough, is exactly what is happening.

4. Fill the aquarium with bubbles, and then gently tilt it at a 45-degree angle. The bubbles will "ride" the heavier carbon dioxide gas out of the aquarium and onto the floor.

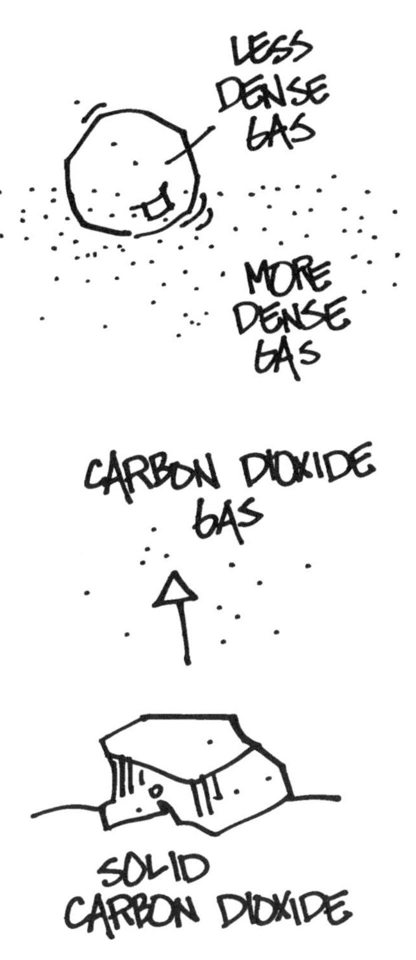

5. Allow the gas to accumulate in the aquarium again and then blow more bubbles. When you have 10 to 15 bubbles floating on the layer of carbon dioxide, gently tip the aquarium back and forth. As the carbon dioxide sloshes back and forth, the motion of the gas will be recorded in the movement of the bubbles on the surface of the gas.

6. Take a bucket and wearing gloves, place a couple of pieces of dry ice in the bucket, and then pour the gas from the bucket into the aquarium when there are bubbles floating on the surface. As the level of carbon dioxide increases, the height of the bubbles inside the container will get higher and higher.

Dancing Bubbles

How Come, Huh?

Dry ice is solid carbon dioxide, a substance that is usually a gas at room temperature. When the dry ice is placed in the tank, it sublimes, which means that it changes directly from a solid to a gas without ever becoming a liquid. As the dry ice changes to a gas (one that is heavier than air, we might add), it starts to fill the tank. Remember that two chunks of matter can't occupy the same space? Same deal here. The carbon dioxide is heavier, so it pushes the lighter air out of the tank. Check out the illustrations to the right.

When the bubbles—full of air—fall into the aquarium, they stop when they hit the layer of heavier carbon dioxide—just like tossing a piece of wood on the water. It just floats. The bubbles look like they are floating because the gas inside the tank behaves like a liquid and is moving constantly.

Science Fair Extensions

15. You can demonstrate the density of the gas—carbon dioxide— and the role of oxygen in combustion at the same time. With the help of an adult, light a votive candle and place it on the edge of the aquarium. Take an empty glass and fill it full of carbon dioxide by scooping it into the aquarium. Gently pour the carbon dioxide directly from the cup on to the flame of the candle, which will extinguish immediately.

16. Set up a relay competition where carbon dioxide is ferried from a main source to an outpost. First one to get the bubbles to overflow is the winner.

Big Idea 2

Objects have many observable properties, including size, weight, shape, color, temperature, and the ability to react with other substances. Those properties can be measured using tools, such as rulers, balances, and thermometers.

Thermometer Rules!

The Experiment

Scientists use a tool called a thermometer to measure temperature. In fact, the name gives away the function. *Therm* translates to heat, and a *meter* is a tool. So, a thermometer would be a tool that measures heat.

This lab will do two things. First, it will demonstrate why tools are more reliable when recording temperature than human touch; and two, we will introduce you to two of the three temperatures scales used in the world today.

Materials

3 #303 Soup cans, empty
1 Celsius/ Fahrenheit thermometer
1 Pair of hands
1 Clock with sweep-second hand
Hot water
Cold water
Ice cubes (optional)
Room-temperature water
1 Assistant

Procedure

1. Place the three #303 soup cans in front of you on the table. Each can should have the top removed and be clean.

2. Fill the first can on the left with hot water from the tap. The second can, on the right, should have very cold water from the tap and even a couple of ice cubes if you can swing it. The third can, between the other two, should be full of room-temperature water.

3. Wrap your right hand around the can with the hot water and your left hand around the can with the ice cold water. Leave your hands wrapped around the cans for exactly one minute.

4. When one minute is up, remove both hands and place them on the middle can at the same time, holding opposite sides. Use the illustration to the right as a guide.

Record the temperature that you feel with each hand in the space provided on the following page.

5. Now, using a Celsius/Fahrenheit thermometer, measure the temperature of each can in both Celsius and Fahrenheit temperatures. If using a thermometer is new to you, simply place the fat end of the thermometer in the water. Leave it there for 30 seconds; then lift it up above the water level and look at the top of the red line. The numbers, written in both temperature scales, will be right there for you to read. Record the data in the space provided on the next page.

Thermometer Rules!

Data & Observations

1. Circle the choice written below in bold that best describes what you felt with each hand as you touched the middle can.

a. The temperature of the middle can felt **warmer, cooler,** or the **same** as the can full of *hot* water when I touched it with my *right* hand.

b. The temperature of the middle can felt **warmer, cooler,** or the **same** as the can full of *cold* water when I touched it with my *left* hand.

2. Describe what you felt when you had both hands on the middle can. ____

____

____.

3. Why would hands be considered poor instruments for recording temperature? ____

____

____.

4. Record the actual temperature reading for each can in spaces provided.

Can	Celsius	Fahrenheit
Hot		
Middle		
Cold		

How Come, Huh?

When you place your hand in cold water, it immediately starts to adapt. It closes down the size of the cells so that heat loss is minimized, coordination is reduced, and your hand becomes less flexible. When you place your hand around the warm can, the circulation in your fingers increases, muscles relax, and flexibility increases. When you grab the middle can, your hands are confused about this new addition to the family.

The hand that was cold now feels a relatively warm can. The hand that was hot now feels a relatively cool can—two hands, one person, two ideas. Curious.

Science Fair Extensions

17. You can repeat the experiment and instead of holding the outside of the cans you can place two different metals, copper and aluminum for example, and then place them on a piece of plastic that is in the middle. You'll have to do some research to find out how this kind of conduction works in the human body.

18. Design another experiment that uses a hot item and cold item but do not tell your assistant what it is if you can help it.

19. Figure out what the Kelvin scale is, who invented it, what it is used for, and how to measure it. Extend the data table that you find on page 48 to include Kelvin measurements as well.

Cubit Catastrophe

The Experiment

If you had lived in medieval Europe, you would have taken your measurements in digits, palms, spans, and cubits. Each of these measurements would have been based on your own personal body dimensions and not a standardized mark.

This lab will do two things. First, it will demonstrate why tools are more reliable when recording length than using portions of the human anatomy, and two, we will introduce you to the two scales used in the world today to measure the length of an object.

Materials

1 Ruler with inches and centimeters
1 Body
1 Friend
Several objects to measure

Procedure

1. First turn to the Data & Observations - A section and fill in the objects that you are going to measure. We have selected a couple and are going to leave the other two up to you.

2. Now that you have selected objects that you are going to measure we are going to ask you to measure them four ways—using

your body, using a friend's body, using the English system of measurement, and using the metric system.

3. The first set of measurements is done using your body and was originally used in Europe to measure lengths. You will immediately see the problem with this kind of tool.

A. Digit: the width of your middle finger
B. Palm: the width of the palm of your hand
C. Span: the distance from pinky tip to thumb tip with fingers spread as far apart as possible
D. Cubit: fingertip to fingertip with your arms spread as far apart as possible

4. Measure each of the items in the data table using your body. Record each measurement in the appropriate space.

Data & Observations - A

Using your body . . .

Item	*Digits*	*Spans*	*Palms*	*Cubits*
1. Book	_____	_____	_____	_____
2. Table	_____	_____	_____	_____
3. Pants	_____	_____	_____	_____
4. ___________	_____	_____	_____	_____
5. ___________	_____	_____	_____	_____

1. Measure each of the items in the data table using your friend's body parts. Then record each measurement on chart B on the next page.

Cubit Catastrophe

Data & Observations - B

Person Number 2

Item	*Digits*	*Spans*	*Palms*	*Cubits*
1. Book	_____	_____	_____	_____
2. Table	_____	_____	_____	_____
3. Pants	_____	_____	_____	_____
4. ___________	_____	_____	_____	_____
5. ___________	_____	_____	_____	_____

2. Now measure the items using the modern English system of inches and feet. When you are done with that, measure using the metric system.

Data & Observations - C

Using a marked measuring stick measure

Item	*English*	*Metric*
1. Book	_____	_____
2. Table	_____	_____
3. Pants	_____	_____
4. ___________	_____	_____
5. ___________	_____	_____

How Come, Huh?

You can immediately see, using the medieval system, that you are going to get a lot of variation in measurement. If I am very tall and design a table based on my cubits and then send the order to the next town to a carpenter who is very short, I will be very surprised—his cubit will be much shorter than mine.

The new English system is much more reliable, but it is difficult to use compared to the metric system. The English system utilizes inches, feet, and yards. There are 12 inches to a foot and 3 feet to a yard. The metric system is based on the unit of 10 and is grounded in a scientific measurement. Hopefully you have had some time to learn your metric system, but if not, this lab will introduce you to a topic that would take several weeks to cover properly.

Science Fair Extensions

20. Invent an original system of measurement for length, mass, and volume that is reliable. You will need to define each unit. Use the units to measure several things and show that the amounts measured can be accurately communicated.

21. Develop a game that teaches the metric system to younger students.

Beakers, Flasks, & Graduated Cylinders

The Experiment

If you are going to be measuring liquids, you will be using beakers, flasks, and graduated cylinders to collect and measure the volume.

This lab will introduce you to each of these three tools. You will also learn to use pipettes, which didn't fit in the already-all-too-crowded title.

Materials

1 250 ml Beaker
Water
1 Bottle of food coloring
1 250 ml Flask
1 100 ml Graduated cylinder
1 1 ml Pipette

Procedure

1. Grab the beaker—this is the short, fat, glass container that looks like a drinking cup with measurements printed on the side. A cartoon bearing some resemblance to this tool is staring at you from the corner of this page.

If you look on the side you will see some numbers. Add water to the beaker until you reach the 100 ml mark. The water level should touch the 100 ml mark but not go over it. Add a couple of drops of food coloring and swirl to make the water easier to see. Draw a picture of what your beaker looks like with the water in it in the Data & Observations section.

2. Next, pour the 100 ml of colored water into the flask—this container looks like a triangle that has been inflated. It has a skinny neck and a big old bottom with markings along the side—cartoon to the right. Draw a picture of what your beaker looks like with the water in it in the Data & Observations section.

3. Finally, pour 80 ml of liquid from the flask into the graduated cylinder. This container looks like a long skinny neck with a collar around the top and a base to hold it up at the bottom. It also has markings along the side—cartoon to the left.

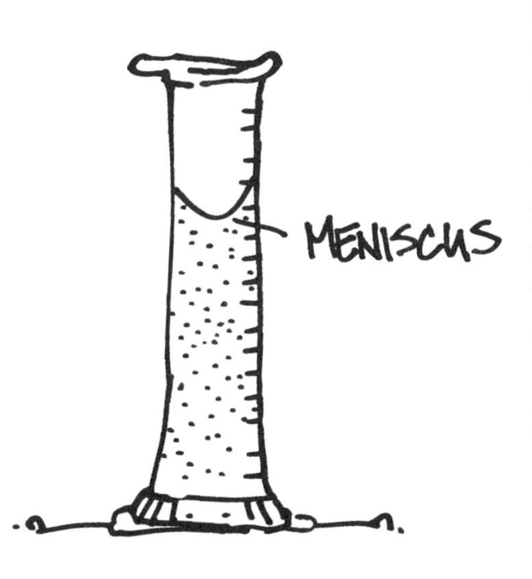

The tricky thing about reading the volume of a graduated cylinder is that the container is narrow enough that a dip forms in the water. This dip or indentation is called a *meniscus.* To determine the true volume of water that is present in the cylinder you have to look at the very bottom of the dip and read the number that correlates to it.

Draw a picture of what your graduated cylinder looks like with the water in it in the Data & Observations section.

4. To use the pipette, squeeze the bulb and insert the nose of the pipette into the water. Release the bulb, and water will be drawn up into the pipette. If you look carefully, you will see that there are four marks along the nose of the pipette. These markings each represent one quarter of a ml. Add 5 ml to your graduated cylinder and draw what you see in the last picture of the Data & Observations section.

Beakers, Flasks, & Graduated Cylinders

Double Pan Weigh In

The Experiment

How much an object weighs is a defining characteristic if you can determine the volume and then density of the object.

To introduce the idea of weight you are going to construct a simple balance and use it to measure the weight of 5 different objects in units called a "paper clip."

Materials

2 5 oz. wax cups
1 Roll of masking tape
1 30 cm ruler
1 Pencil
1 Box of paper clips
Assorted objects to weigh (your choice)

Procedure

1. Place a loop of tape, sticky side out, on the bottom of each wax cup and then fix them to the opposite ends of the ruler as pictured below.

2. Place the pencil under the ruler at the center point, 15 cm, and adjust the cups until the instrument balances.

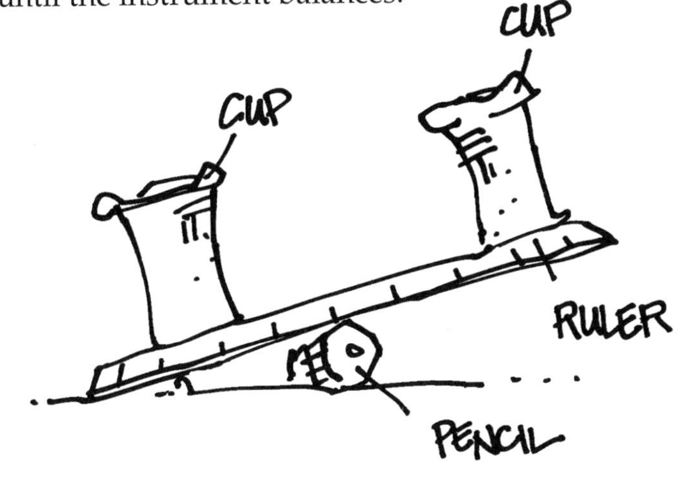

Double Pan Weigh In

3. Select 5 small objects that you find around the ranch to weigh. Logic dictates that the objects ought to be able to fit in the cup.

Place the first object in one of the cups and add paper clips, one at a time until the balance tips. Record the number of paper clips it took to balance the object in the space provided in the 15 cm column.

4. Move the pencil so that it is resting under the 20 cm mark. Then either add or remove paper clips so that the balance balances again. Record that number in the 20 cm column below. Repeat the process after moving the pencil to the 10 cm mark.

5. Repeat the procedure for the other four items you chose.

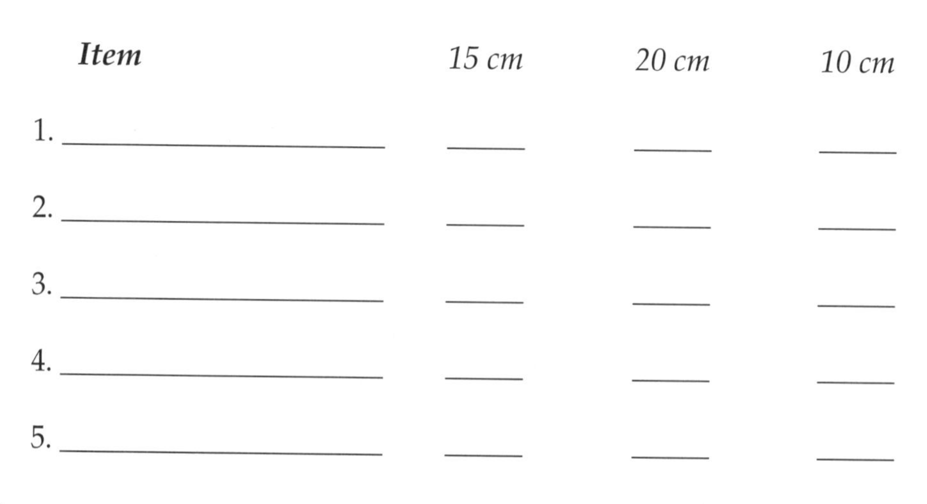

Data & Observations

Item	*15 cm*	*20 cm*	*10 cm*
1. ____________________	_____	_____	_____
2. ____________________	_____	_____	_____
3. ____________________	_____	_____	_____
4. ____________________	_____	_____	_____
5. ____________________	_____	_____	_____

How Come, Huh?

When you placed the pencil under the center of the ruler, you were creating a simple machine to measure the weight of the object that you placed in the cup. You added paper clips, our unit of measure, until the scale tipped; and then you recorded that number.

By moving the pencil closer to the object weighed, you were actually making it easier for the object to be lifted by the cup full of paper clips. This is evidenced by the fact that all of the numbers in that column were lower than the numbers in the 15 cm column.

By moving the pencil farther away from the object weighed, you were actually making it harder for the object to be lifted by the cup full of paper clips. This is evidenced by the fact that all of the numbers in that column were higher than the numbers in the 15 cm column.

There are two lessons to take away from this lab. One, all matter not only takes up space but also has weight. And, two, you must make sure that your instrument is accurately calibrated so that you get an accurate measurement of the weight of an object. Being a little off in either direction will affect the measurement.

Science Fair Extensions

22. Design and build a scale that measures the weight of an object. Be sure to incorporate a method to calibrate (zero out) your scale as well as accurately measure the weight of the object placed in the scale.

23. Design and build a scale that specifically measures either gas or liquids. Show how the scale can be calibrated, and determine what limitations your scale has, if any.

Bird Bonz

The Experiment

This activity gives you an opportunity to learn about two things. First, it rounds out the labs that explain Big Idea #2 with a lab about specific chemicals reacting in specific ways. Second, you will also become acquainted with the minerals found in bird bones and eggs that cause them to be hard, and you will learn about the structure of bird bones.

Materials

4 Fresh chicken wing bones, meat removed
1 16 oz. bottle of distilled, white, household vinegar
2 12 oz. plastic cups
1 Fresh egg
1 Spoon

Procedure

1. Remove any remaining meat and cartilage—the soft, whitish gray matter near the joints—from the bones. Break one of the bones in half and observe the inside. In the interest of good hygiene, you should wash your hands well after picking at these bones.

2. Put the other three bones in the first cup and cover them with vinegar. Set them in a place where they will remain undisturbed, as it will take several days for the bones to react completely with the vinegar.

3. Next, put the unbroken fresh egg into the second cup. Pour enough vinegar over the egg to completely cover it, then either cover the cup or replace the vinegar as it evaporates. It will take 18 to 24 hours for the egg and vinegar to react completely.

4. After 24 hours, use the spoon to gently remove the egg from the glass. Set it on the table. Carefully push on the egg and observe what used to be the shell. After a few days, remove the wing bones and examine them. Try to bend them and see if they snap as easily as they did when you first started the experiment.

Data & Observations

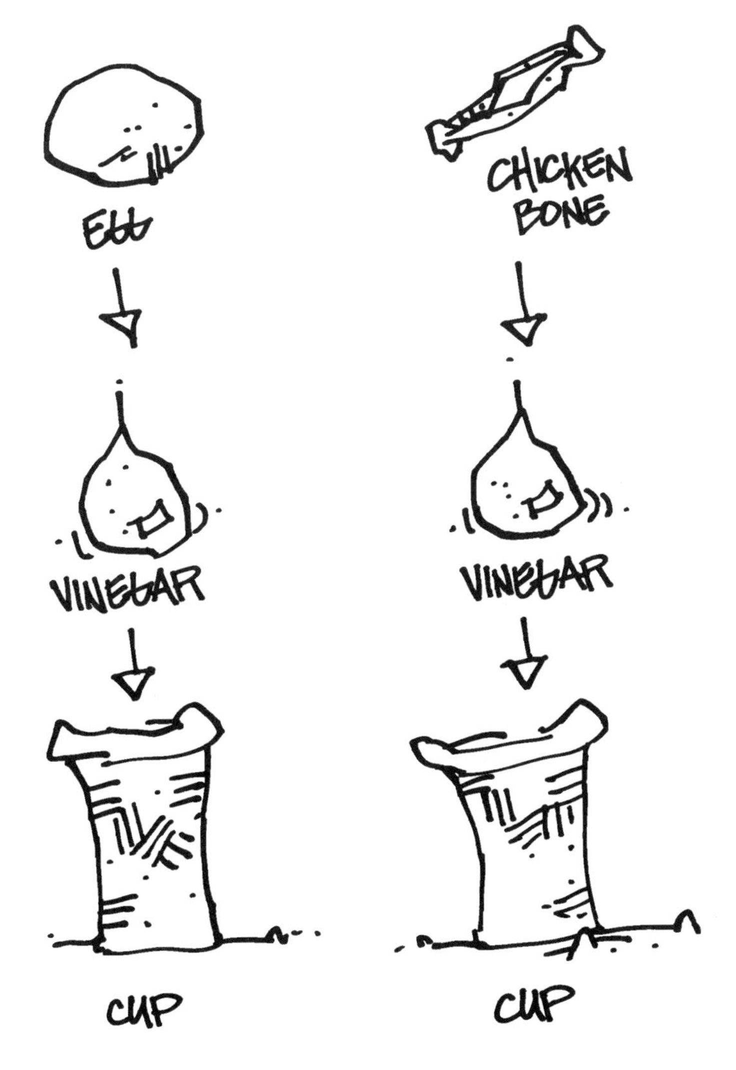

Bird Bonz

1. Describe the color and the hardness of the chicken bone before and after you placed it in the vinegar. ______________________________

____

____.

2. Describe the color and the hardness of the surface of the egg before and after you placed it in the vinegar. ______________________________

____

____.

How Come, Huh?

Bones and shells are hard because they incorporate a mineral called calcium into their structure. This is why you always see ads telling you to drink your milk and eat your cheese if you want strong bones. Milk and cheese are rich in calcium.

When you placed the egg and the bones in the vinegar, the vinegar started to attack the calcium and react with it. The calcium was leached or stolen from the eggshells and bones. When this happens, the structure of the bone and shells is weakened. It's kind of like taking bricks out of a house. You take enough of them and the wall gets real mooshy. Same thing here.

Science Fair Extensions

24. Under the supervision of an adult you can experiment with other DILUTE acids. Muriatic (hydrochloric) acid is available from pool supply companies and sulfuric acid can be purchased through outlets available in the Yellow Pages™.

25. Get a nutrition guide and see what other foods contain calcium. Don't forget to look at your dark green, leafy vegetables as well as dairy products. Cut up some samples and place them in vinegar and see how they are affected by the reaction.

Big Idea 3

Matter can exist in three different states: solid, liquid, or gas. Matter changes state when the temperature goes up or down. The point of change, independent of the volume of the sample, is predictable and is recorded as the freezing and boiling points.

Cubes to Clouds

The Experiment

The three states of matter are solid, liquid, and gas. Most substances change from one state to another at a very predictable temperature.

Changes from solid to liquid or liquid to solid are called the melting and freezing points, respectively. They are identical. Changes from liquid to gas or from gas to liquid are called the vaporization or condensation points, respectively, and they are also the same.

This lab will allow you to observe, measure, and record the three states of water and the transition points between those changes.

Materials

1 1000 ml beaker or quart saucepan
Ice cubes
Clock
Water
1 C° Thermometer
1 Hot plate or stove (Adult supervision needed)
1 Metal soup can, #303
1 Ruler

Procedure

1. Fill the beaker half full with ice cubes and then add water to the level of the ice cubes. Insert the thermometer, gently swirl it around a couple of times and record the temperature on the 0 line of the Temp. column of the data table on the next page.

2. Turn the hot plate or stove on with adult supervision and record the temperature for every minute in the spaces provided in the data table below. Continue to heat the ice-water mixture until the water has boiled for three minutes or more.

3. Once you have observed the transitions from solid to liquid to gas and recorded the temperature in the table below, graph the data that you collected on the next two pages.

Data & Observations

Time	Temp.	Time	Temp.
0		16	
1		17	
2		18	
3		19	
4		20	
5		21	
6		22	
7		23	
8		24	
9		25	
10		26	
11		27	
12		28	
13		29	
14		30	
15		31	

Cubes to Clouds

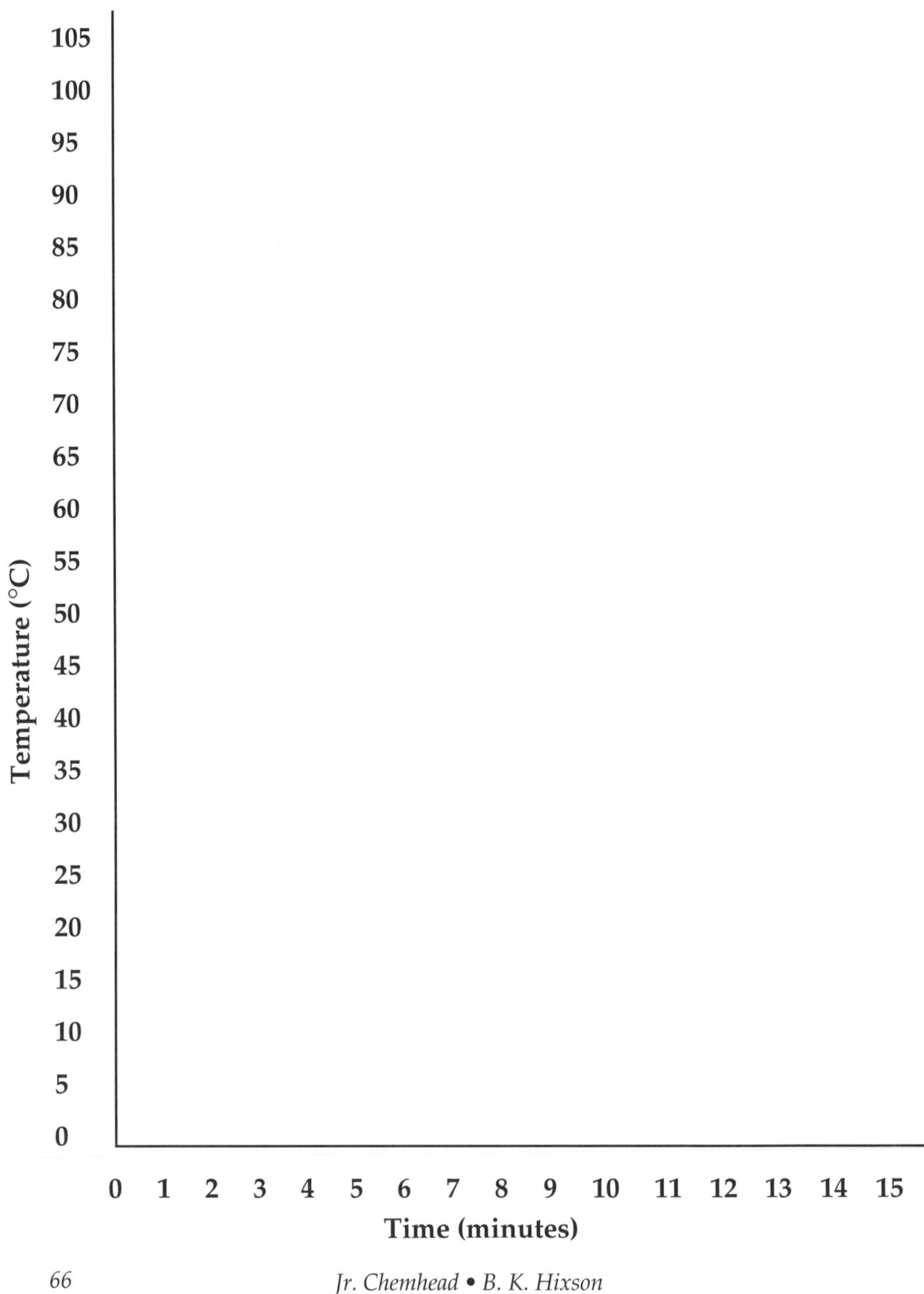

16 17 18 19 20 21 22 23 24 25 26 27 28 29 30

Time (minutes)

Cubes to Clouds

Procedure

4. To continue the process of exploring states of matter take a metal soup can and fill it with ice cubes and then add water until the can is full. Place a thermometer in the can and record the temperature of the water below.

5. Place the can in a warm spot and observe what happens to the outer sides of the can. Record the temperature of the water when you start to see drops of water forming on the outside of the can. This water appears on the outside of the can because water in the air, called humidity, comes in contact with the cold surface of the can and condenses there. The same process creates clouds in the sky.

Data & Observations

The starting temperature for the can was _____°C.

The moisture appeared on the can at _____ °C.

How Come, Huh?

When you graphed out the data, you should have noticed that the temperature of the ice water did not change very much as the ice was melting. This is represented by a fairly flat line starting out your graph.

Once all of the ice had melted and changed to liquid water, the temperature started to rise. It continued to rise until the water approached the boiling point.

As the water started to boil, the graphing line once again leveled off meaning that the temperature of the solution remained the same. This is how chemists identify the transition points of different compounds. Once the temperature line levels off, the transition point has been reached.

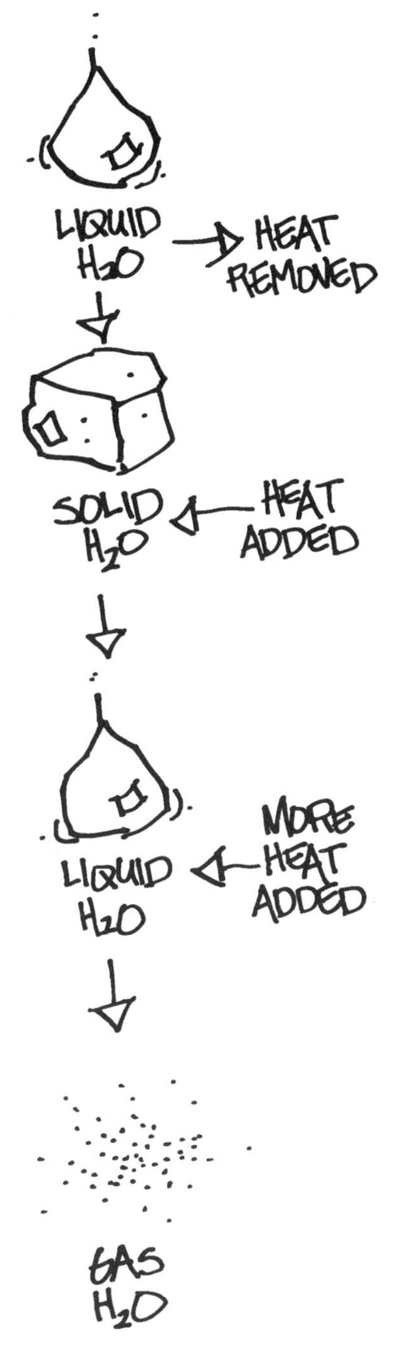

Science Fair Extensions

26. Experiment with recording and determining the melting point of several soft solids, like butter, lard, or Crisco™.

27. Experiment with recording and determining the boiling point of several liquids of your choice. Be sure to have an adult approve your choices—stay away from flammable liquids like gasoline, acetone, mineral spirits, and other liquids that may produce toxic or flammable fumes.

28. Explore the idea of sublimation. Find out what it is and what it has to do with the states of matter and how they transition. With an adult to guide you, explore dry ice and caffeine—two compounds that sublimate very easily.

Swiss Cheese Candles

The Experiment

Making your own candles and taking advantage of the states of matter will create some fun investigations of matter. When hot, liquid wax is poured into a container filled with ice cubes, the ice will take up space and the wax will harden into interesting shapes. Add a wick and tah-dah... you have created a unique, one-of-a-kind, Swiss cheese candle. Add a gift tag and you may put a smile on someone's face for a special gift occasion.

Materials

1 Electric skillet (Adult supervision needed)
Water
1 Metal soup can, #303
1 Cube of paraffin
1 Crayon pieces
1 Small wax cup
1 Heavy cotton string for wicking
1 Ice cubes
1 Oven mitt

Procedure

1. With the supervision of an adult, plug the electric skillet into the wall and adjust the setting to medium high. Keep in mind that every skillet will be a little different so feel free to adjust the temperature. Add enough water to fill the bottom of the pan about one-half-inch deep.

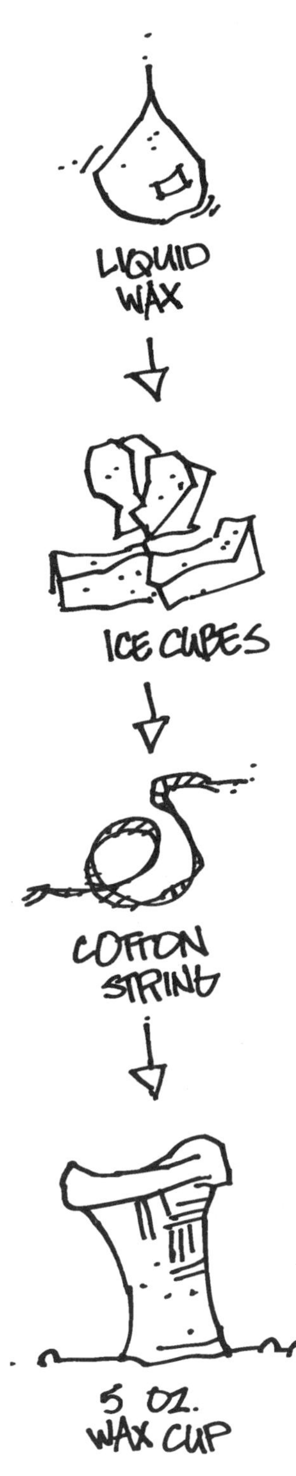

2. Place the soup can in the heating water and add chunks of paraffin wax to the can as well as pieces of colored crayon if you are looking to add some zing to your final product.

3. Take the wax cup and place one end of the cotton string in the bottom. Add a couple of ice cubes and wind the string around them. Add a couple of more ice cubes, each time wiggling the string in and around the cubes. You should have at least 1 inch of string, more is fine, left over when you fill the carton full of ice cubes.

4. Put the oven mitt on and remove the can of melted paraffin from the electric skillet. Pour paraffin into the wax cup and over the ice cubes. The wax will almost immediately set up and solidify, but you are going to want to leave the wax cup sitting overnight so that eventually all of the ice will melt.

5. The next day you can pour off the water from the melted ice cubes. Carefully remove the paper of the wax cup from the candle, and you will be able to see where the ice cubes were once present.

6. If you time this just right, you have your Christmas present, Mother's or Father's Day gift, or simply a fun table decoration for Cheese Day, of which there has got be a least one, especially if you live in Wisconsin.

Swiss Cheese Candles

Data & Observations

Draw a picture of your Swiss Cheese Candle in the space provided below.

How Come, Huh?

Matter can be defined as anything that takes up space and has mass. Frozen water (ice) takes up space and has mass. When hot wax is poured over the ice cubes, the wax takes the shape of the container and surrounds the ice. When the wax hardens and the ice melts, bubbles of empty space are formed and create the "Swiss cheese–looking" candle.

Science Fair Extensions

29. The same kind of process creates what are called trace fossils. These are fossils that get coated in volcanic ash, sediment, or some other casting materials and when the original fossil decomposes, traces of the fossil are left behind. Create a lab to demonstrate this idea.

See-Thru Fat

The Experiment

Fat molecules, some of them anyway, have some very interesting optical properties that you can explore. When some materials change state, they also take on different visual characterisitics. In this lab you will explore a compound that does just that.

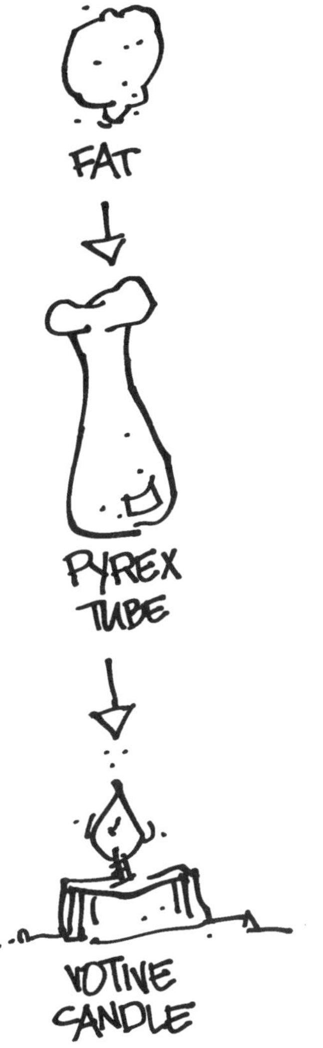

Materials

1 Test tube, Pyrex™
1 Test tube holder
1 Clump of fat (butter)
1 Knife, table
1 Pair of goggles
1 Votive candle
1 Book of matches (Adult supervision needed)

Procedure

1. Using the table knife cut a clump of butter from a stick. Place a clump of fat in the bottom of your test tube. Do your very best to get it to the bottom without greasing up the sides as it slides down.

2. Hold the test tube up to this page and, looking through the fat, try to read the top paragraph on this page.

See-Thru Fat

3. Don your goggles. With the supervision of an adult, light the candle, insert the tube in the tube holder, and gently heat the fat. You will notice as it gets warmer and warmer that it liquefies and becomes transparent.

4. Once the fat has liquefied, hold the tube up to the top paragraph of the page and try to read it. Record your observations for both conditions in the space below.

Data & Observations

Draw a picture of what the text in the paragraph looked like when the fat was cool, again when the fat was warm, and a third time as the fat cooled again.

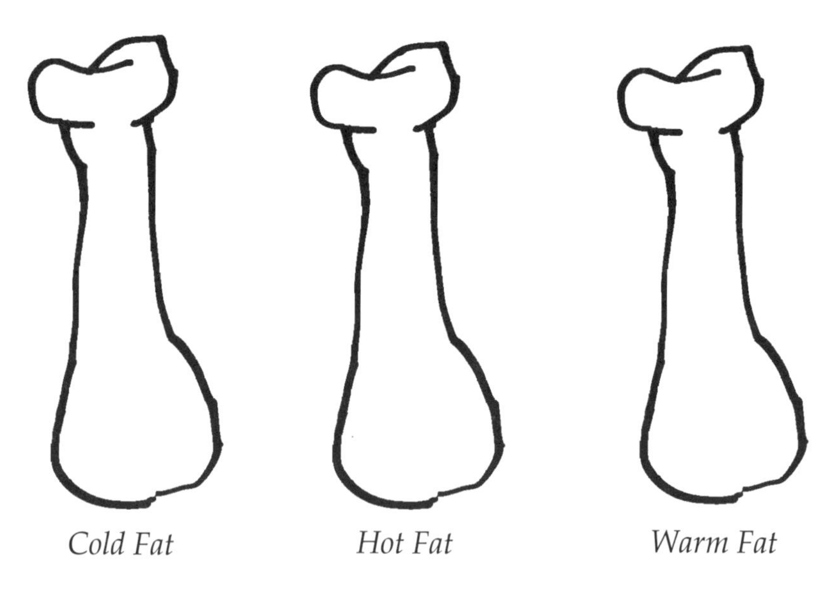

How Come, Huh?

Fat molecules are extremely long and have numerous sites that are free and available to hook with other molecules. When the fat is room temperature, these long molecules are all tangled and connected to one another making the fat appear opaque. You can't see through it.

When the same substance is heated, the molecules start to move around with more and more energy, basically untangling themselves—apologies to the chemists of the world for that explanation—becoming transparent. Cooks call this process clarifying butter. You are separating the milk solids—the top portion of white gunk—from the clear, yellow oily portion of the sample.

Finally, the end product is translucent at the bottom—the yellowish section, and the top, white, portion is opaque once again. The only way to get back to your original butter consistency is to whip the two layers together.

Science Fair Extensions

30. You can repeat the experiment with other kinds of fat: bacon grease, lard. Then compare the results that you get.

31. Modify the experiment and mix varieties of fat with one another to see if all fat behaves the same.

32. Try heating sugar and see if there are any similarities between liquefied fat and sugar that has been heated to a liquid state.

The Ice-Cube Roundup

The Experiment

Sometimes the temperature of a substance can be affected by things other than heat. When two chemicals are mixed together and they absorb heat from their surroundings, they are called *endothermic*, but if they produce heat, they are called *exothermic*.

In this lab, salt will be added to water, causing it to refreeze. We are going to take advantage of this reaction to capture a couple of wayward ice cubes. Using nothing more than a piece of cotton string and a little chemistry savvy.

Materials

1 Ice cube
1 Length of string
1 Packet of salt
1 5" diameter pie tin

Procedure

1. Rinse the ice cube under the water for just a second and then place it in the pie tin. Place the string directly on top of the ice cube. Do your very best to catch it. Wrap it under, around, speak with it sternly if you must, but no touching.

2. When your frustration level is tapped out, open the salt packet, lay the string across the top of the ice cube, and sprinkle a little bit of salt over the surface of the ice cube. Be sure to sprinkle salt on the string as well.

3. Count to five and lift the loose end of the string—and you too can be an accomplished ice-cube fisherman.

4. Once you have caught one ice cube, go for the record. Lay as many ice cubes together as your supply will allow. Then wiggle the string in around and through the assortment, and salt the entire collection. As you do this, you may want to be careful when you salt—some folks have a special ability to get the ice cubes to freeze to the pie tin.

5. As your string grows, see if you can get ice cubes that you have already caught to catch other ice cubes even without the string coming in direct contact.

How Come, Huh?

As the ice cube sits at room temperature, it begins to melt, and a layer of water is formed on the surface of the cube. When you place the string on the ice cube, nothing happens, but it does get slightly wet in the water layer.

Sprinkling salt on the string and the ice cube causes the salt to dissolve in the thin layer of water on the surface of the cube. When the salt atoms break apart (dissolve), the process takes heat away from the water on the surface of the ice cube and in the string, lowering the temperature. When the temperature gets low enough, the water refreezes connecting the string to the ice cube, resulting in a successful ice-cube roundup.

The Ice-Cube Roundup

Science Fair Extensions

33. This is not so much an extension of science as a fun activity that you can do with your friends—have an ice-cube relay. Give each kid a cotton string and line them up in two lines at one end of the competition area. Have a pile of ice cubes at the other end. When the starter says, "Go," the kids race down to the pile of ice cubes, line up and salt as many of them as possible, and race back to the line. The team with the most ice cubes wins.

34. There are several commercial brands of ice melter available on the market. These are chemicals that folks spread on their sidewalks and driveways to remove snow and ice. Try these and see if there is a successful alternative to table salt.

35. With the help of an adult, substitute dry ice for regular ice. Do you need salt? Do you need water? How could a lab like this be completed? What safety precuations would you need to take using dry ice?

Big Idea 4

The smallest unit of matter is called an atom. There are roughly 100 different atoms organized in a chart called the Periodic Table of the Elements. This table describes specific characteristics about each element that allows scientists to identify them.

Chem Shorthand

The Experiment

Chemists work with chemicals that are often written as abbreviations, a kind of scientific shorthand, using symbols from an alphabet called the Periodic Table of the Elements. It is similar to the alphabet you learned when you were a little kid, but this one is designed just for chemicals. Just like the 26 letters in our alphabet can be arranged to make words, combinations of the 108 elements in the Periodic Table can be arranged to make every known chemical. It was important to learn the alphabet when you were a kid so you could read and write. It is also important to be familiar with the names and symbols of the elements from the Periodic Table, so you can read and understand chemical equations and formulas.

Materials

1 Pencil or pen
1 Periodic Table of the Elements
1 Imagination

Procedure

Take 10 minutes to create as many words as you possibly can using the symbols of the elements listed below. For example, you can combine H and I to spell HI; or Ne, C and K to spell NeCK. Use any symbol as often as you like and use them multiple times in a single word. Let your imagination run wild!

Be sure to copy the symbols exactly as they are written in the space below. This is one time that you won't get in trouble for mixing upper case and lower case letters together. List the words in the box on the next page.

H	**He**	**Li**	**B**	**C**	**N**	**O**	**F**	**Ne**
Na	**Mg**	**Al**	**Si**	**P**	**S**	**Cl**	**Ar**	**K**
Ca	**Mn**	**Fe**	**Co**	**Ni**	**Cu**	**Zn**	**Br**	**Kr**
Sr	**Ag**	**Sn**	**Au**	**Hg**	**Pb**	**Ra**	**Th**	**U**

Shorthand Words

Chem Shorthand

1. Select 5 words from your list and translate them. To do this, match the symbols from your Shorthand Words with the elements they represent in the table below. For example, HI is made up of two symbols, ***H***, which is the abbreviation for hydrogen, and ***I***, which is the abbreviation for iodine. You would translate HI like this: HI Hydrogen, Iodine

H	Hydrogen	He	Helium	Li	Lithium
B	Boron	C	Carbon	N	Nitrogen
O	Oxygen	F	Fluorine	Ne	Neon
Na	Sodium	Mg	Magnesium	Al	Aluminum
Si	Silicon	P	Phosphorous	S	Sulfur
Cl	Chlorine	Ar	Argon	K	Potassium
Ca	Calcium	Mn	Manganese	Fe	Iron
Co	Cobalt	Ni	Nickel	Cu	Copper
Zn	Zinc	Br	Bromine	Kr	Krypton
Sr	Strontium	Ag	Silver	Sn	Tin
Au	Gold	Hg	Mercury	Pb	Lead
Ra	Radium	Th	Thorium	U	Uranium

Chem Words	*Translations*
a. ____________	____
b. ____________	____
c. ____________	____
d. ____________	____
e. ____________	____

2. Have a parent or classmate check your translations. When you both agree that they are correct, translate the actual chemical formulas that are listed below. Break apart the word and translate each element on a separate line. For example, HI would be translated like this:

HI — Hydrogen ______
Iodine ______

Chemicals — *Translations*

a. NaOH ______
______
______

b. HOH ______
______

c. CaClCl ______
______
______

d. SiO ______
______

e. SnNOO ______
______
______
______

Science Fair Extensions

36. Create your own word game using the Periodic Table of the Elements as the basis.

Iron Inquiry

The Experiment

Magnetism is another characteristic of certain elements that is easy to test for and define. If you have studied magnets at all, you have an idea that objects that contain iron respond to magnets and that cobalt will respond to magnets under the right circumstances.

In this particular lab, you are going to use the magnetic characteristics of iron to separate it from salt using a magnet. It will be a lot easier than the pick-and-sort method; it also demonstrates that salt is not magnetic.

Materials

1 1 oz. Bottle iron filings
1 1 oz. Bottle salt
1 Pie tin
1 Craft stick or straw
1 Ceramic magnet
1 Paper towel

Procedure

1. Pour a capful of iron filings into the pie tin and add a capful of salt directly on top. Using the craft stick or straw, stir the two compounds together to form a mixture.

2. The trick now is to separate the two compounds from one another. You could take a magnifying glass, a pair of tweezers, and accomplish the task in a couple of days—or you could wrap the magnet in the napkin.

3. With the magnet in the napkin, run the magnet through the mixture of salt and iron. The magnet should attract the iron filings but leave the salt in the pan. After a couple of seconds, you will have a bearded napkin. Remove the magnet to the tabletop, slide the magnet out of the napkin and the iron filings will fall to the tabletop and be officially separated from the mix.

How Come, Huh?

I am pretty sure you have this one covered, but a magnet produces a magnetic field that reaches out from the ends of the magnet and penetrates almost anything. When this magnetic field comes in contact with an object that has iron in it, it will attract that object.

In this particular case the magnet attracted the iron filings but did not attract the salt. Because of this different response to the magnet these two compounds were able to be separated from one another.

Science Fair Extensions

37. You can repeat the experiment and get a little more sophisticated by adding several compounds to the mixture, and you will still be able to get out the iron.

38. Take salt, iron, and sand. You can remove the iron with the magnet. How do you get the salt out of the sand. Head to the ocean for the answer.

39. Some cereals advertise that they are iron fortified and they truly are, with real, non-digestible iron. Take several breakfast cereals and run a magnet through them to see if you can find the iron filings.

Sulfur Bombs

The Experiment

Rotten-egg gas, also known as hydrogen sulfide, commonly escapes Mother Nature's bowels via volcanoes, gas wells, coal pits, sulfur springs, and the gastrointestinal exit ports of individuals who have eaten large quantities of fried onion rings. You may be more familiar with the smell as it emanates from an egg that you lost during the annual Easter hunt in spring and found just before Christmas—not a pleasant smell.

Odor can be used as an identifying characteristic for some elements, specifically, sulfur compounds that have a tendency to smell like rotten eggs.

In this experiment, you will be generating hydrogen sulfide gas by mixing iron filings with an acid in a cup. This reaction produces a memorable odor, something resembling rotten eggs. Definitely a face wrinkler that should be shared with a close friend or cherished sibling—and when you do, they are going to want to known what you have done.

Materials

1 1 oz. Bottle of iron filings
1 1 oz. Bottle of distilled white vinegar
1 Straw
1 5" Pie tin
1 Adult supervision needed

Procedure

1. Pour a small pile of iron filings, about half the size of a dime, in the pie tin.

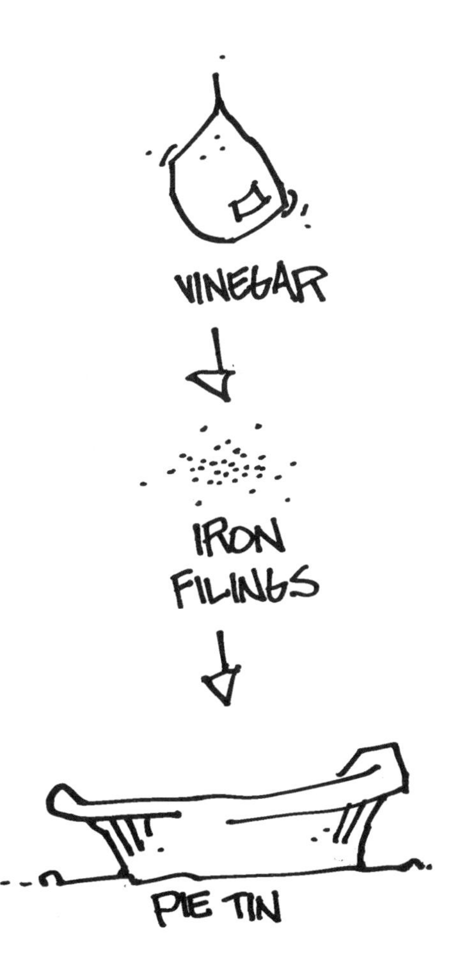

2. Review wafting in the Safety Section on page 18 of this book. You should not directly inhale the gas from the pie tin or hold the pie tin directly under the nose of anyone. Use proper wafting technique. In high concentrations, hydrogen sulfide gas can be poisonous, so be sure an adult is present when you do this experiment.

3. Insert the straw in the bottle of vinegar. Place your finger over the open end and trap a couple of drops of liquid. Dribble the vinegar directly on the filings. Lean over and carefully waft the odor that is produced by the reaction.

4. After the your eyes start to water, rinse out the pie tin and toss it in the garbage can.

How Come, Huh?

The iron filings react with the vinegar to produce a gas called iron sulfide, our aforementioned source of the odor du jour. The smell that you wafted was produced primarily by the element sulfur and demonstrates rather forcefully how odor can be used an identifying characteristics of some of the elements of the Periodic Table.

Sorting Sugar & Salt

The Experiment

Shape is a distinguishing characteristic when it comes to identifying different kinds of compounds. This translates over to geology where cleavage and fracture are two very useful ways to describe the shapes of minerals that present themselves as crystals. We also find it in physics with simple machines and in all the life sciences.

To build on these ideas, we are going to have you take a peek at two very common food products, salt and sugar, and examine the shape of each.

Materials

1 Packet of salt
1 Piece of black paper
1 Packet of sugar
1 Hand lens or magnifying tripod
1 Colored pencil, white

Procedure

1. Empty the salt packet out onto a piece of black paper or anything that will provide a lot of contrast to the white salt crystals. Using the hand lens or tripod for an assist, draw the crystals, as you see them, in the space on the next page, and describe the shape of this compound.

2. Empty the sugar packet out on to a piece of dark-colored paper or any other object that will provide contrast to the white sugar crystals. Draw the crystals, as you see them, in the space on the next page.

Data & Observations

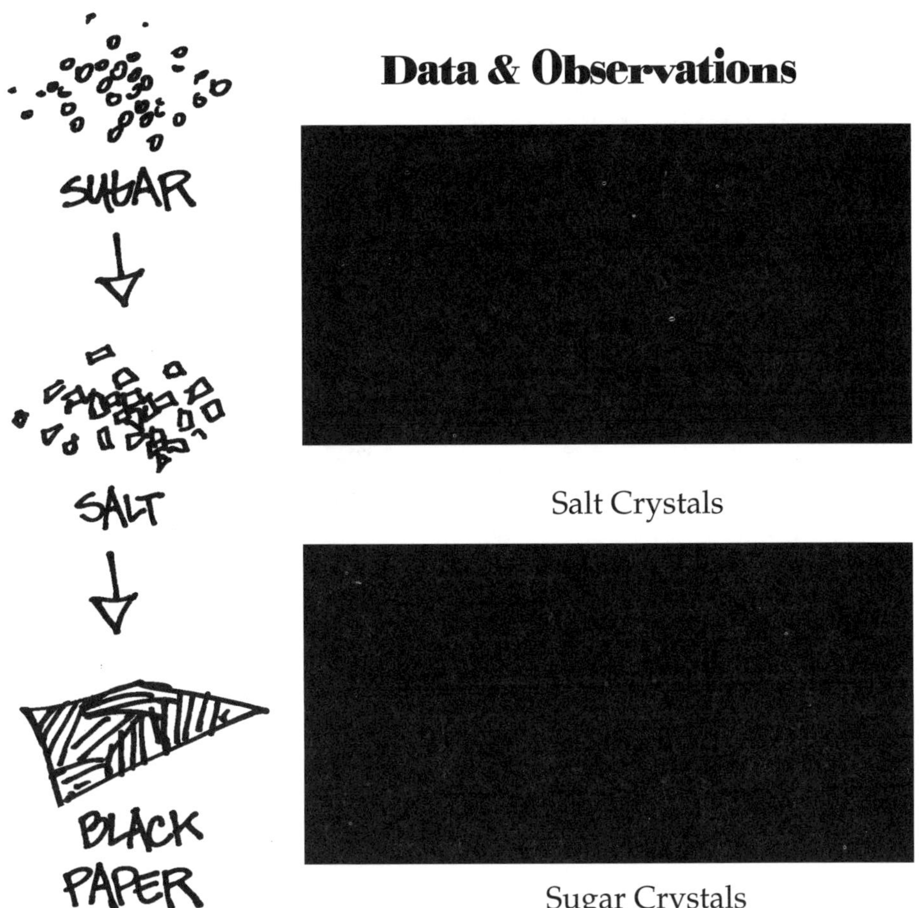

Salt Crystals

Sugar Crystals

How Come, Huh?

The shape of the crystal is dictated, to a degree, by the shape of the atoms and molecules that make up the compound. Salt is square and sodium chloride atoms bond in a cubic pattern, sugar is less regular in shape. The large crystal will always give away clues to the arrangement of the molecules.

Science Fair Extensions

40. Compare other crystals: copper sulfate, cobalt chloride, as well as common minerals.

Decomposing Carbon

The Experiment

And finally, color can also be used as an indicator to identify elements as well as to signal that a chemical reaction has taken place. Sugar, in the minds of most folks, is a white compound. However, it is primarily made up of carbon. Carbon, in its elemental state, is very black.

Materials

1 Eyewash station or sink
1 100 ml Beaker
1 Pie tin
1 Pair of goggles
1 Pair of gloves
1 1 oz. Bottle of sugar
1 1 oz. Bottle of sulfuric acid
Adult supervision

Procedure

1. **WARNING: Sulfuric acid is nasty stuff. You do not want to use it if you are a kid. It puts holes in synthetic carpets instantly, makes cotton clothing look like cheesecloth in a heartbeat, and causes blindness if accidentally splashed in eyes. Have an adult demonstrate this experiment for you in A WELL-VENTILATED AREA.**

2. Go outside or to a well-ventilated area. Invert the pie tin so that it produces a heat sink. Place the 100 ml beaker upside down in the middle of the pie tin.

3. Put on your goggles and your gloves. Fill the beaker to the 20 ml mark with granulated sugar. Carefully add 20 ml of concentrated sulfuric acid to the sugar. Pour to the 40 ml mark on the beaker.

4. You will have to wait a least a minute or two for the reaction to really get going. After a while, the whole concoction will start to smoke, and the sugar will turn from white, to yellow, to brown, to black. When it reaches the black stage, it is actually sustaining a chemical burn and oxidizing.

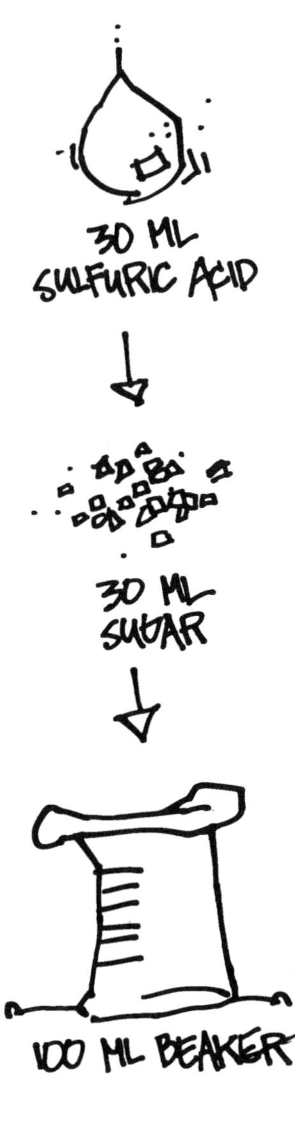

5. When the reaction is complete, you will notice that the beaker is hot. DO NOT TOUCH THE BLACK SNAKE THAT HAS GROWN OUT OF THE BEAKER. It is coated with sulfuric acid and will burn your skin, make holes in your clothes, and all sorts of other reactions.

6. To dispose of your snake, pick it up with a plastic baggie, place it in the baggie, sprinkle a generous amount of baking soda on it, and give it a toss.

How Come, Huh?

The sulfuric acid oxidized the sugar. In simpler terms it cooked it so fast that it burned it to a crisp. As the sugar cooked, it expanded and trapped air inside the carbon structure. Speaking of carbon, the black color is the carbon found in the molecule itself. Pretty cool stuff.

Science Fair Extensions

41. Find an old piece of polyester carpet and have an adult pour a dash of sulfuric acid on it to see what happens.

BS Fire Extinguisher

The Experiment

Liquid soap is added to a Toobe that contains baking soda solution. When the vinegar is also added, it finds the baking soda and they react with one another. This reaction produces carbon dioxide, a gas, which is released into the solution. Being lighter than the liquid, the gas starts to rise up to the top of the cup. As the gas gets to the surface and tries to escape, the soap catches it and forms a foam. The gas is trapped inside the liquid.

This is an example of two different chemicals reacting with one another to produce a new compound, carbon dioxide gas. It is a very specific reaction and can be repeated infinitely, supporting the Big Idea stated at the opening of this chapter.

Materials

1 1 oz. Bottle of baking soda
1 16 oz. Bottle of vinegar
1 1 oz. Bottle of liquid soap
1 5" Pie tin
1 Toobe or other container
1 Straw
1 Votive Candle
1 Book of Matches (Adult supervision needed)

Procedure

1. Put the Toobe or other container in the pie tin. Add 4 ounces of water to the Toobe, two caps of baking soda powder, and a big dash of liquid soap. Mix all of the contents thoroughly with the straw.

2. Quickly add 4 ounces of vinegar to the Toobe and observe what happens. The foam that you see rising out of the Toobe is carbon dioxide gas trapped in soap and water.

3. Clean your Toobe out and repeat the first step again but <u>without the soap</u>. This time we are more concerned about retaining the carbon dioxide gas and using it to perform an experiment.

4. Have an adult light a match and slowly lower it into the Toobe as far as possible without getting a burn. Observe how long the flame burns.

5. Throw away the match and slowly add 2 ounces of vinegar to the Toobe, which will fizz and fill with carbon dioxide gas. Have an adult light another match and slowly lower it into the Toobe. If the match is extinguished, that means there is no more air. The point in the Toobe at which the match is extinguished is also the level of the carbon dioxide in the Toobe.

6. With the help of an adult, light the votive candle. Hold the candle near the top of the Toobe and gently tip the Toobe and pour the contents of the container out on to the candle flame and observe what happens.

BS Fire Extinguisher

Data & Observations

1. Draw a picture of the foam in the box below.

2. Describe what happened when an adult lowered the match into the Toobe after the vinegar and baking soda had mixed. ______________________

____

____

____

________________________________.

3. Describe what happened when you poured the carbon dioxide out of the Toobe on to the candle flame. ___________

____

____

____

________________________________.

4. How do these two experiments confirm that there was a new compound formed inside the Toobe? ____________________________

____

____

____.

How Come, Huh?

When baking soda and vinegar mix, they produce a new compound called carbon dioxide gas. If you could see regular oxygen and carbon dioxide molecules, they would look something like the illustration to the right. The carbon dioxide molecule is quite a bit bigger than the oxygen molecule.

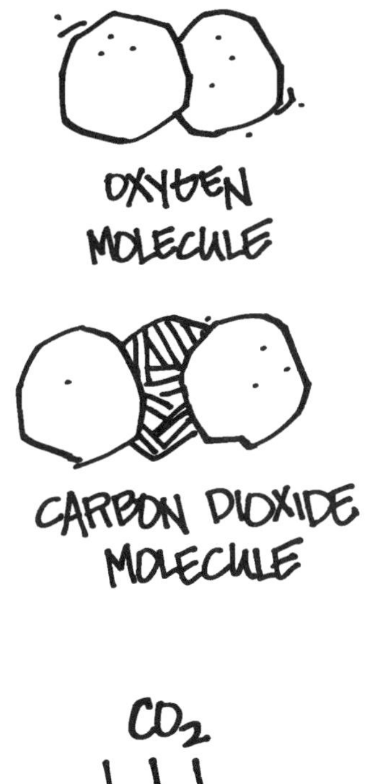

When an adult placed the burning match in the Toobe full of air, it simply continued to burn—demonstrating no change. When you mixed the chemical and then inserted another match that was immediately extinguished, that told you that the environment inside the Toobe had changed dramatically.

Finally, when the Toobe was tipped and the heavy carbon dioxide gas had a chance, it escaped. It fell directly on top of the candle flame pushing the air aside—no air, no combustion; no combustion, no flame.

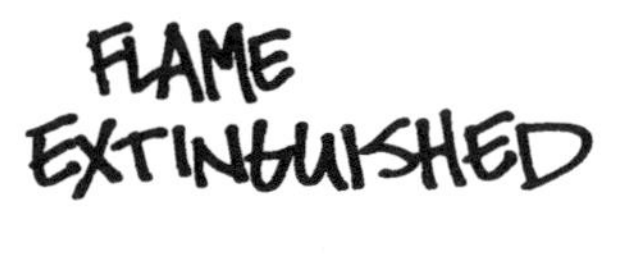

Science Fair Extensions

42. Create a demonstration with an adult where you will take an aquarium or other clear container, place lit candles at different heights in the aquarium, and record the amount of time it takes for each candle to extinguish.

43. Use soap bubbles floating on dry ice to demonstrate the same reaction that you got in Science Fair Extension 42.

Big Idea 5

Elements can combine or bond with one another in groups of two or more, producing molecules. When this happens, a new compound is formed that has its own, unique set of characteristics.

Marshmallow Molecules

The Experiment

You are learning to read chemical formulas. A formula simply tells you what kinds of atoms are in the molecule and how many of each kind there are.

A molecule is the name given to a substance that has two or more atoms hooked together. For example, in the formula for water H_2O, the H stands for hydrogen. The little tiny 2 immediately following the letter H tells you that there are two hydrogen atoms in this molecule. The O stands for oxygen. If there is no number after the letter, that means there is only one of that atom in the molecule. Another example would be $CaCl_2$. This is calcium chloride, a type of salt that is tossed out on your sidewalk in the winter to melt the ice and snow. This formula tells us that there is one calcium (Ca) atom, and there are two chlorine (Cl) atoms in every calcium chloride molecule.

In this lab activity, you will build models of molecules by reading the formula and then mooshing toothpicks into colored marshmallows to get an idea of how the molecules may appear.

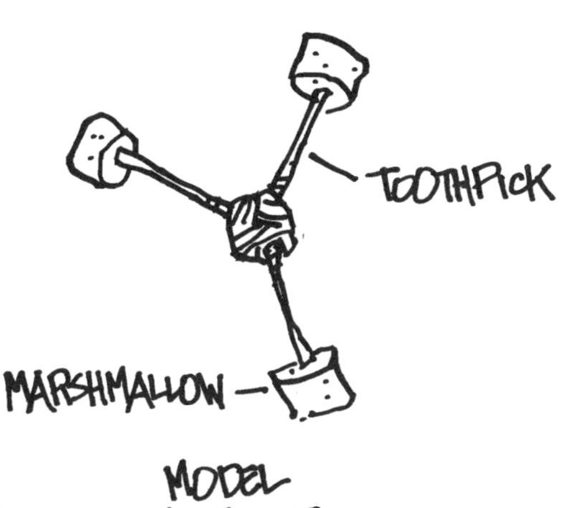

Materials

1 Pencil
1 Box of toothpicks
1 Bag of marshmallows, multicolored

Procedure

1. Ten molecular formulas are listed on page 98. The first thing to do is translate each formula: Next to the formula, write the names of the elements. If there is more than one of each atom in the molecule, write that number after the element. The first translation, for H_2O, has already been completed to help you get started.

Marshmallow Molecules

Formulas		*# Atoms*	*Translations*
a.	H_2O	2	Hydrogen
		___	Oxygen
b.	H_2	___	Hydrogen
c.	$CaCl_2$	1	___
		___	Chlorine
d.	CH_4	___	___
		___	___
e.	CO_2	___	___
		___	___
f.	H_2SO_4	___	___
		___	___
		___	___
g.	NH_3	___	___
		___	___
h.	Zn_2SO_4	___	___
		___	___
		___	___
i.	O_2	___	___
j.	$C_6H_{12}O_6$	___	___
		___	___
		___	___

2. Using your translations, marshmallows, and toothpicks, build models of each molecule and then draw a picture in the spaces provided. If you have two or more of each atom in the molecule, be sure to use the same color marshmallow.

Data & Observations

H_2

$CaCl_2$

H_2O

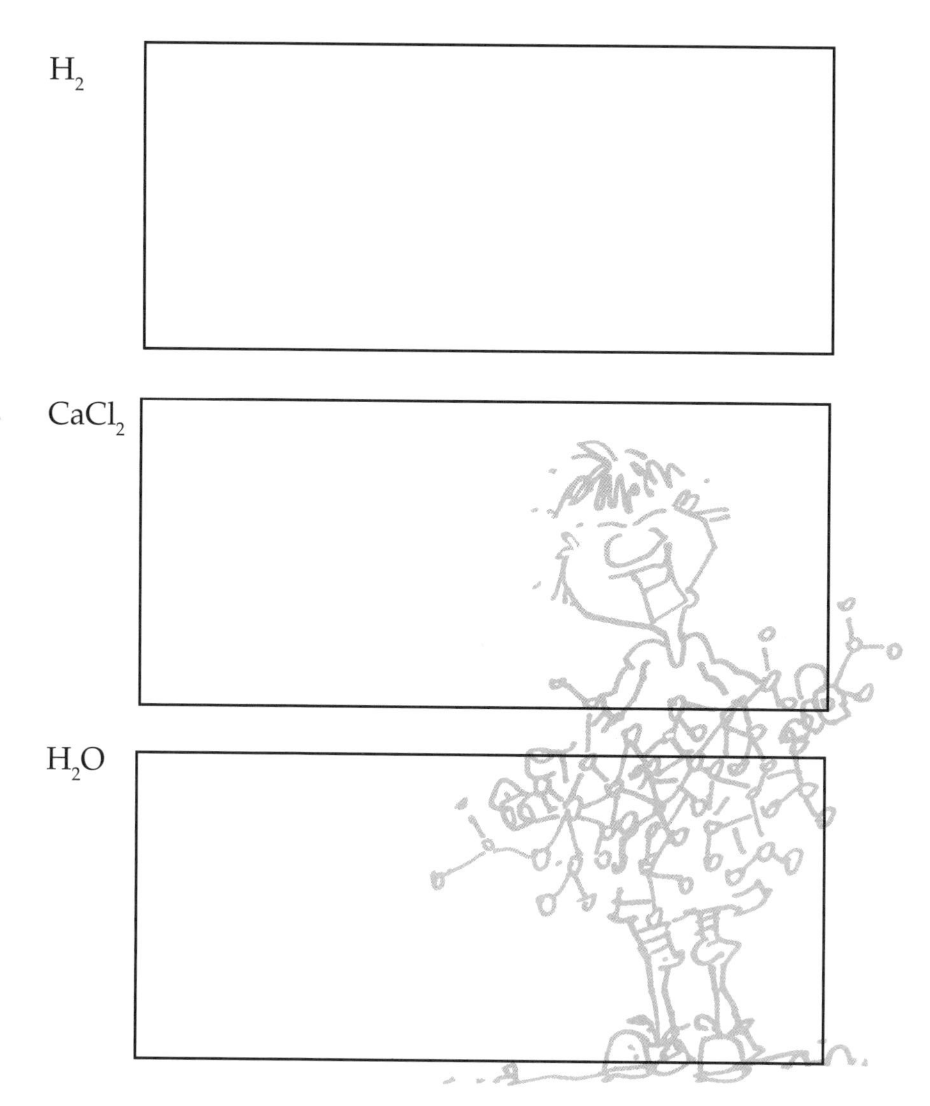

Baking-Soda Cannon

The Experiment

Change of state is one of the identifying characteristics of a chemical change. In the case of this lab a solid—baking soda, and a liquid—vinegar, are mixed together to produce a gas called carbon dioxide. Because this is all done inside a closed container the gas that is released increases the pressure inside the tube to the point where the stopper shoots off the end of the tube and into the air.

Materials

1 16mm by 150mm Test tube
1 #0, Stopper, solid, rubber
1 Square of toilet paper, single ply
1 1 oz. Bottle of baking soda
1 1 oz. Bottle of vinegar
1 Pair of goggles (recommended)

Procedure

1. Take a section of toilet paper and pour a pile of baking soda the size of a quarter into it. Fold the toilet paper in half several times until it looks something like a plug. Wedge the toilet paper wad between the ring and pinky fingers of your left hand.

2. Hold the test tube in your left hand also, using your thumb and forefinger to hold the test tube, and pour about half an inch of vinegar into the bottom of the tube.

3. Wiggle the wad of toilet paper into the top half of the tube and plug it securely with the stopper. Be sure that you are pointing the tube toward

the ceiling or away from yourself or anybody else.

4. Put on your goggles and shake the tube up and down quickly about 5 to 8 times. The vinegar will saturate the baking soda and carbon dioxide gas will be released inside the tube.

There will be a very quick reaction, and the stopper will shoot into the air when the pressure inside the tube is great enough.

Be sure that you are pointing the tube up and away from yourself and others to avoid the risk of shooting someone with the stopper and also covering them with a piece of wet, acidic toilet paper full of wet baking soda.

How Come, Huh?

Baking Soda reacts with the vinegar to produce large amounts of CO_2 gas. The gas pressure builds up to the point where the stopper can no longer contain it, and the stopper shoots off the top of the tube. When the pressure inside the tube is released with the removal of the stopper, other things like liquids, wet toilet paper, and gas come zinging out of the tube and into the air.

For chemical formula enthusiasts . . .

$$NaHCO_3\ (s) + CH_3COOH\ (l) \rightarrow Na(CH_3COO)\ (aq) + H_2CO_3\ (aq)$$

$$H_2CO_3\ (aq) \div \quad H_2O\ (l) + CO_2\ (g)$$

Science Fair Extensions

44. Design a cannon loaded with a measured amount of vinegar and baking soda powder and mount it in a cannon mount of your design so that it will shoot a predictable distance.

Steel Wool Sparkler

The Experiment

Another set of clues that a chemical reaction has taken place is the production of heat and also light.

In this lab you are going to light steel on fire with a candle flame. Impossible, you think, but the reality of the situtation is that the kindling point—the temperature that iron catches on fire—is actually lower than paper. The trick is getting enough oxygen to the reaction to keep it going.

Materials

1 Pair of goggles (recommended)
1 Candle, votive
1 Book of matches
1 Pie tin
1 Test tube holder
1 # 16 nail
1 00000, Steel wool pad
1 Fire blanket (recommended)
Adult supervision

Procedure

1. Put your goggles on and place the candle in the center of the pie tin. Ask an adult to light the candle.

2. Place the nail in the test tube holder and then insert the nail into the flame of the candle. Roll the nail around inside the flame of the candle and do your very best to get it to catch on fire. After 30 seconds place the HOT nail inside the pie tin, next to the candle.

3. Take the piece of steel wool and "tease" the fibers into a large ball to expose the steel to plenty of oxygen. The bigger, the better. Clip one side of the ball of steel wool into the test tube holder and then place the steel wool ball in the candle flame.

4. The steel wool will ignite and burn and smoke. Be sure to keep holding the burning steel wool over the pie tin. When the reaction is done, you can release the wool from the clip and throw the leftovers in the garbage can.

How Come, Huh?

When a single strand of steel wool comes in contact with the candle flame, there is enough heat for the steel to reach what is called the kindling point—the temperature when a substance bursts into flames. Given the fact that there is plenty of oxygen available to the steel wool, it continues to burn and burn. The nail, on the other hand, reaches the kindling point but does not have enough oxygen exposed to a large enough surface area so there is no combustion.

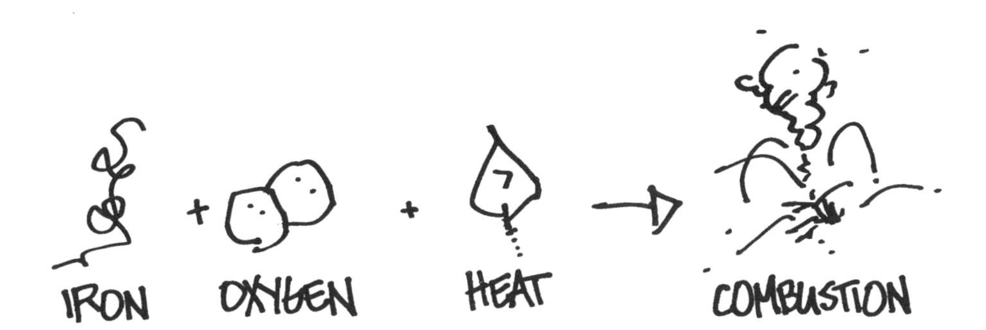

Envious Pennies

The Experiment

Color is another way to help identify a possible chemical change. In this reaction copper metal is going to react with household vinegar—acetic acid—to produce a new compound, copper acetate. The identifying characteristics is the change in appearance of the penny. It goes from copper to green—no envy necessary.

Materials

3 Paper napkins
3 Copper coated pennies
1 1 oz. Bottle of acetic acid
Water
3 Baggies, ziplock, plastic
1 Box of crayons

Procedure

1. Fold each of the napkins into a square. Soak one in water, one in vinegar, and leave one dry.

2. Place one penny inside each of the three napkins, place those in baggies, and leave them overnight.

3. Examine the pennies the next lab period and draw your observations with crayons in the circles in the spaces provided on page 106.

Data & Observations

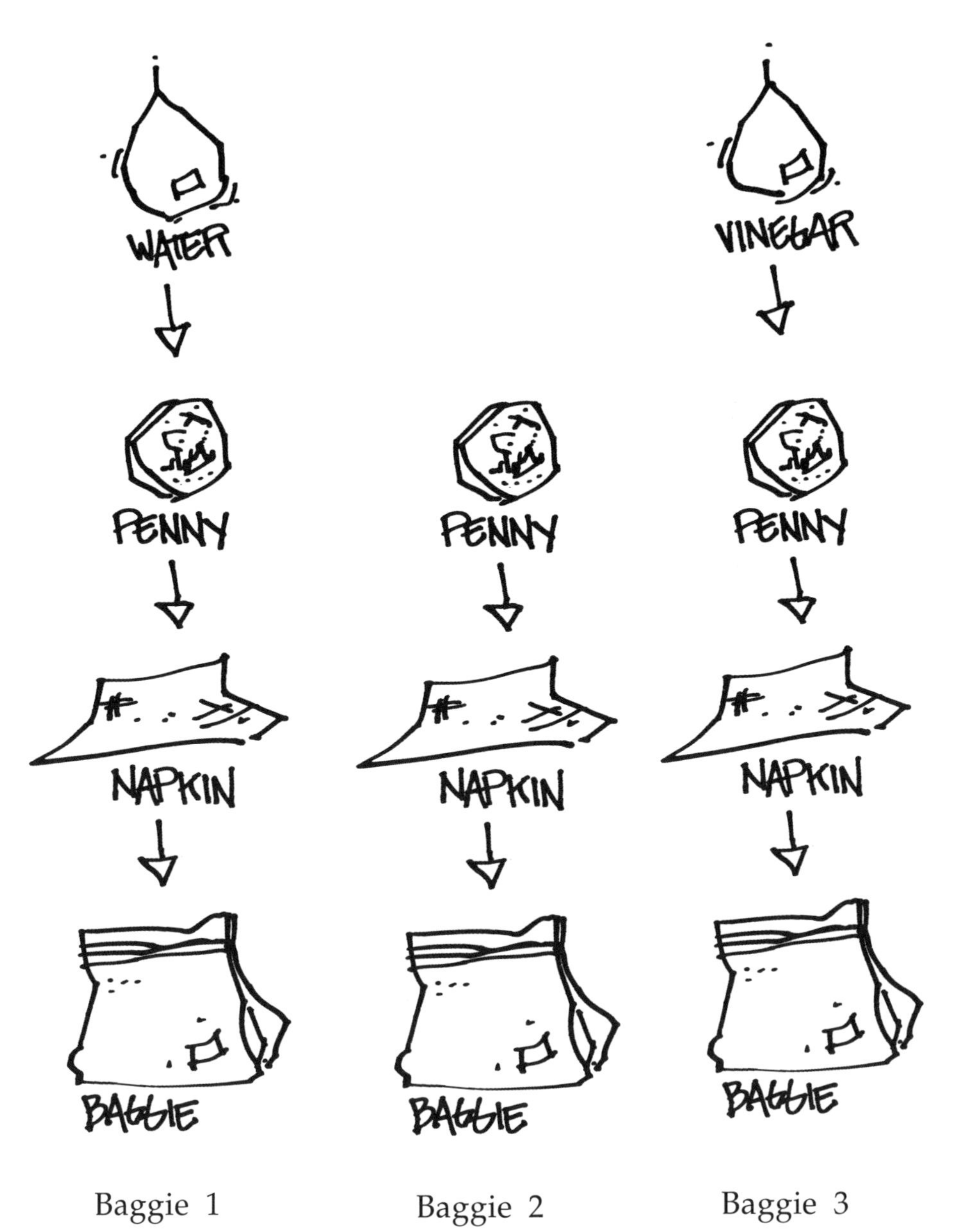

Baggie 1 Baggie 2 Baggie 3

Envious Pennies

Data & Observations

Draw a picture of the pennies before and after you have conducted the experiment.

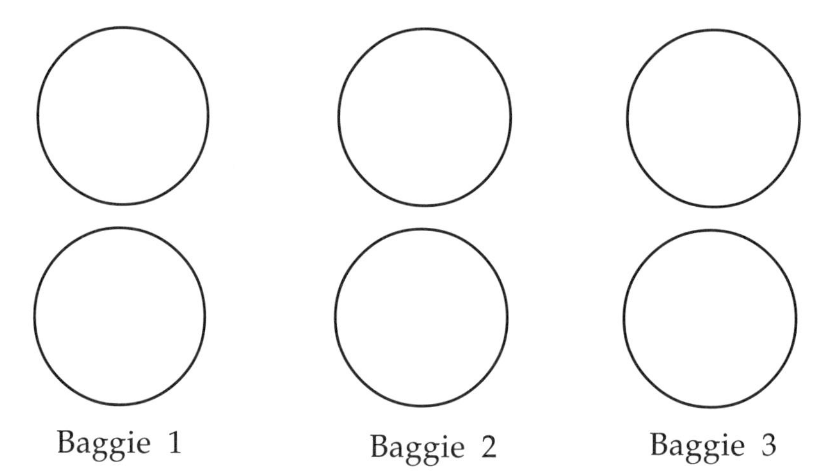

How Come, Huh?

Copper is added to vinegar producing copper acetate, a greenish coating that forms on the surface of the penny. For those of you who like chemcial equations . . .

$$Cu\ (s) + 2CH_3COOH\ (l) \rightarrow Cu(CH_3COO)_2\ (s)$$

Science Fair Extensions

45. Anything special in the copper pennies or will any old kind of copper work just fine? Repeat the experiment with copper tubing, copper wire, native copper, and copper cooking untensils.

46. Do a little research and find other sources of the acetate ion and combine them with copper pennies to see what reaction you get.

Mrs. Stewart's BBQ Garden

The Experiment

This next reaction produces crystals by evaporation. When the crystal-growing solution is poured on the briquettes, they soak up the liquid. The water in the charcoal then slowly evaporates into the air. As it evaporates, it leaves behind the salts that were originally dissolved in the solution as beautiful, and let us forewarn you, *extremely delicate* crystals.

Yes, but what does it all mean in the real world? When you find the real world, let us know—until then focus on your chemistry. Another indicator of a chemical reaction is the production of a new compound. Here salt, bluing, water, and ammonia are mixed together and produce a new, chemically distinct, compound.

Materials

1 Piece of sponge, old sock, or rag
1 Pie tin
1 Bottle of crystal-growing solution
1 Hand lens
1 Pair of goggles

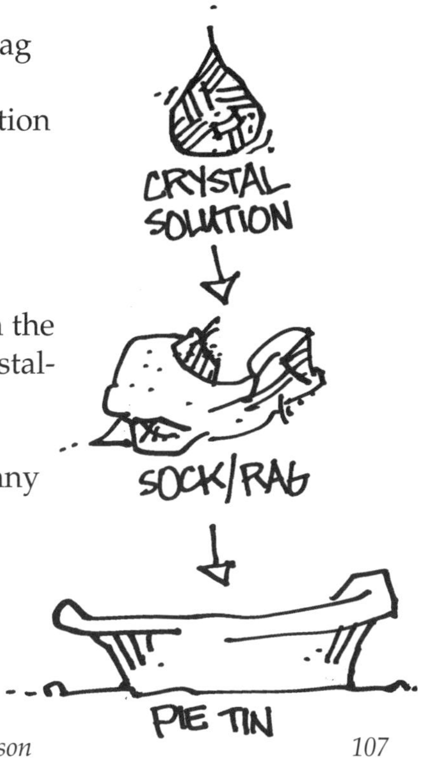

Procedure

1. Place the sponge or old sock in the pie tin, and pour the entire bottle of crystal-growing solution over the sponge.

2. Place the pie tin in a warm, sunny location so that the solution will evaporate. The crystals will begin to appear in one to two hours and will continue to grow until all of the liquid has evaporated.

CRYSTAL SOLUTION
SOCK/RAG
PIE TIN

Mrs. Stewart's BBQ Garden

3. The briquettes will start to sport a collection of very delicate, powdery crystals that will collapse if you touch or even breathe in their general direction—definitely no sneezing.

Data & Observations

Draw top-view pictures of your crystals at 1 hour, 3 hours, 24 hours, and 48 hours.

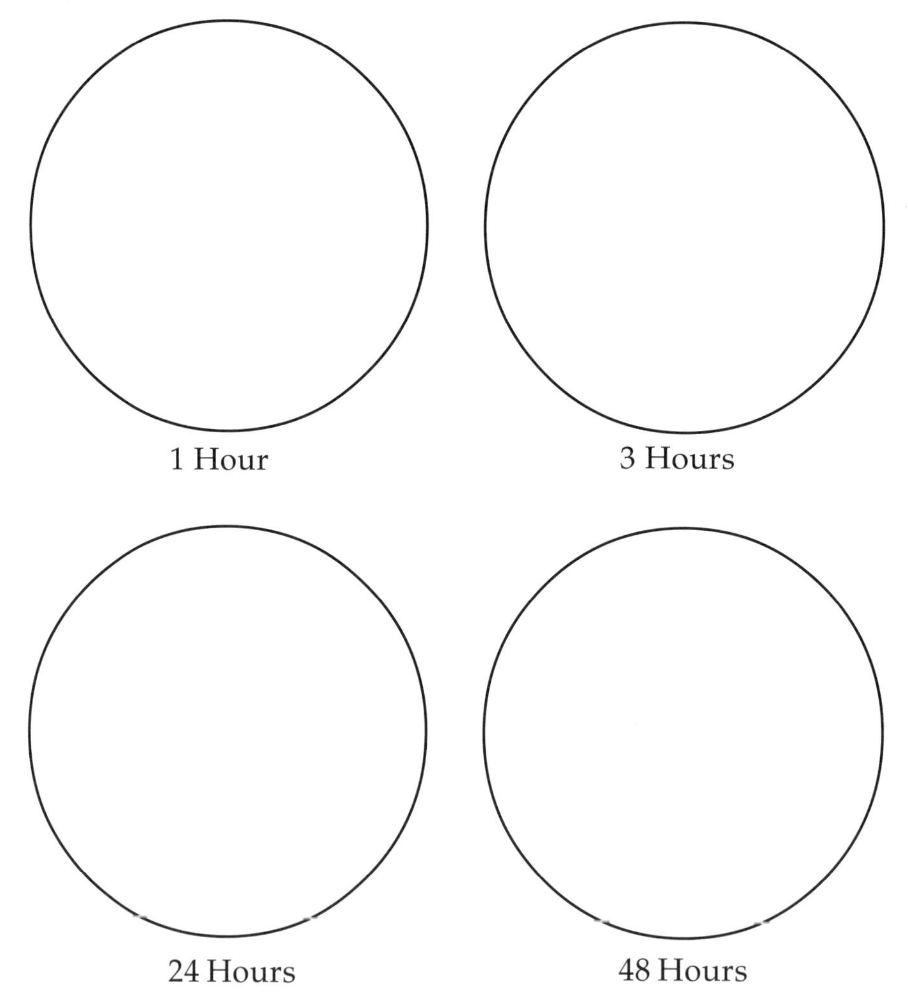

How Come, Huh?

The recipe that we are using to grow these crystals has been around for a long time. It incorporates salt, water, ammonia, and ferrous ferric hexacyanate, also known in washtub circles as laundry bluing, a whitener that is added to clothes.

Science Fair Extensions

One word of caution as you make your own crystal solution: Avoid snorting fumes from the ammonia directly. They do nothing to improve your personality.

47. If you are in the mood to mix a larger batch of the same solution to grow crystals for everyone in your extended family, use the following recipe:

50 ml Table salt
10 ml Ammonia
100 ml Water
50 ml Laundry bluing

Add everything to a large bowl and stir. Pour the contents on a large sponge, or (and this is strictly off-the-record) these crystals will grow on any porous material. Try variations on this recipe, add or subtract portions, see if you can figure out what makes it tick.

48. Try chunks of coal, pieces of soft wood like fir or pine, or old gym socks. To add some color to your crystals, put drops of food coloring on the sponge or substitute material right after you add the solution.

Big Idea 6

A physical change is different from a chemcial change and can be identified when matter goes through a change in shape, size, or state.

Simply Physical

The Experiment

There are several parts to this lab because we are attempting to get this physical vs. chemical thing squared away with a single lab. Hang in there and bear with us.

When two chemicals come in contact with one another and form a new compound, there is a significant change. Heat is given off or absorbed, light may be produced, or perhaps a color changes, a smell is produced, or a new solid, liquid or gas is produced. Any of a number of things could happen. When something undergoes a physical change, it remains the same chemically. It just has a different size, shape, or physical state. For example . . .

Materials

1 Egg, fresh
1 Bottle of vinegar, white
2 Plastic baggies
1 Sheet of paper
1 Book of matches
1 Bottle of sodium chloride
Water
1 Pile of ice cubes
1 Soup can, empty
1 Hot plate or stove
1 Piece of wood
Adult supervision

Procedure

The best way to learn about physical versus chemical change is to give you numerous examples of both.

1. Take a fresh egg and drop it into the kitchen sink from a height of 2 feet. Most eggs will not survive a drop of that height and if you pour out the contents you will see that the egg was smooshed, the shell was cracked—we have a *physical change*.

Simply Physical

The reason why is that the eggshell is still an eggshell, it is just in a lot of smaller eggshell pieces.

2. Place several of the eggshell pieces in a baggie and add a dash of vinegar. Observe very carefully what happens to the eggshells as they are attacked by the vinegar. You will see small bubbles forming on the eggshell. Those are bubbles of carbon dioxide. The vinegar is reacting with the calcium in the eggshells and forming a new compound. This is a *chemical change*. The eggs are becoming something new and different from eggshells.

3. Nab a piece of paper and tear it in half. This is a *physical change*. You have two smaller pieces of paper, but they are still paper.

4. Have an adult light the paper on fire. Observe what happens. The paper changes color, heat is produced, light is produced, an odor is produced—we see a solid changing to a gas. If you are thinking *chemical change*, move ahead two squares and take another turn.

5. Find the sodium chloride—this is ordinary table salt—and add it to a baggie. Not much of a change, just a new container. Now add water to the baggie, zip it closed, and shake it up to dissolve the salt. You might be tempted to say that there was a chemical reaction between the water and the salt. However, before you succumb to that temptation, all you did was *physically change* the salt from a visible crystal to one that is invisible to the naked eye. The way you did this was by dissolving it in water.

6. Ice cubes are placed in a clean soup can. Ice is the solid form of water. With the supervision of an adult, place the soup can on a hot plate or stove and crank it up. The ice will melt from a solid state to water, a liquid state, but it is still water. That is a *physical change*. The water will continue to heat until it starts to boil and form water vapor—water in a gas state but still water. This is another *physical change*.

7. Finally, take a piece of wood and break it in half. Physical or chemical change? *Physical.* Take a match and light the wood on fire, and you have a chemical change complete with new colors, light, heat, change of state, and odor. Complete the data table below.

Data & Observations

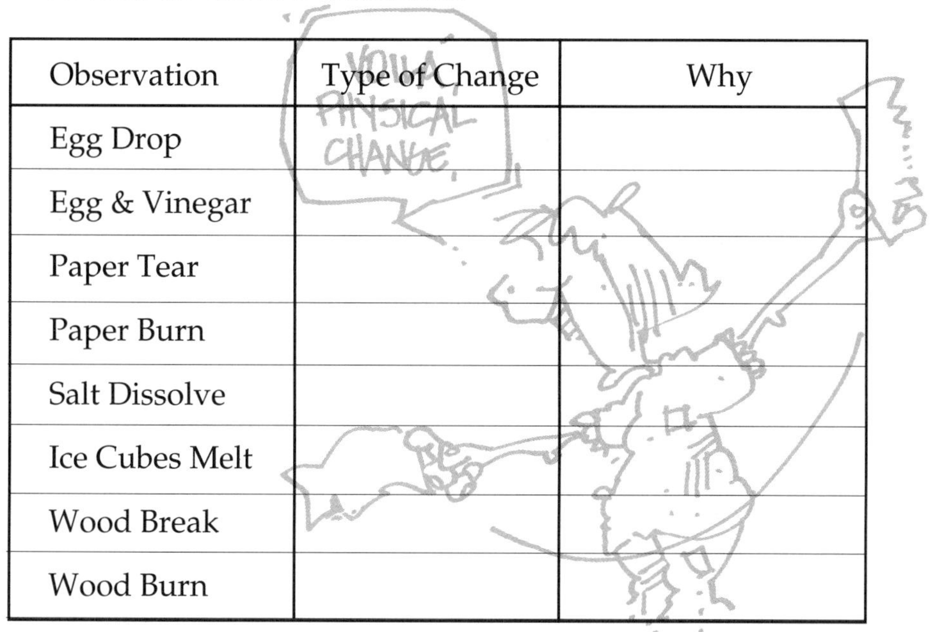

Observation	Type of Change	Why
Egg Drop		
Egg & Vinegar		
Paper Tear		
Paper Burn		
Salt Dissolve		
Ice Cubes Melt		
Wood Break		
Wood Burn		

Science Fair Extensions

49. Create your own physical change/chemical change puzzle for friends and see if they can determine what kinds of changes take place on your lab table.

Eco Peanut Puzzle

The Experiment

If you were to dump a couple of spoonfuls of salt into a cup of water and stir until the salt disappeared, some folks might be tempted to guess that a chemical change had occurred when, in fact, it is a physical change. The salt molecules don't react with the water; they simply dissolve into it and break apart into very tiny, invisible-to-the-naked-eye, salt molecules that float around. Going from big to small but remaining the same chemically is a physical change.

You are going to start with two different liquids and add packing peanuts made out of two different kinds of material. Both are completely different and react differently when they are placed in each of the two liquids.

Materials

2 5" Pie tins
5 Polystyrene packing peanuts (available at local mail co.)
5 Cornstarch packing peanuts (available at local mail co.)
1 2 oz. Bottle of acetone
Water
1 Pair of gloves
1 Pair of goggles

Procedure

1. You are going want to perform this lab in a well-ventilated room, wearing gloves and goggles.

2. Fill one pie tin with enough acetone to cover the bottom about a quarter of an inch deep. Add 1 polystyrene peanut to the pie tin and watch to see what happens when it comes in contact with the acetone. Save one peanut for the next step.

3. Put the remaining polystyrene peanut in your mouth and suck on it. Try your very best to get it to dissolve.

If you are successful, congratulations—you have a very unusual metabolism, and we would highly recommend going to see a doctor at your very earliest convenience. If the peanut does not dissolve, spit it out and save it for later. Record your observation in the space provided.

4. Now, take a cornstarch peanut and put it in the acetone. Roll it around and try to get it to dissolve. When you are done, pop another one of the cornstarch peanuts in your mouth (DO NOT USE THE PEANUT THAT WAS IN THE ACETONE), and see if you can get it to dissolve. Record your observation in the space provided.

5. Add enough water to cover the bottom of the second pie tin a quarter of an inch deep and add a cornstarch peanut to that liquid. Record your observation in the space provided. Finally, take the styrofoam peanut that you spit out on the table and place it in the water. Record your observations.

Eco Peanut Puzzle

Data & Observations

1. Fill in the data table as you experiment. Enter the words "dissolved" or "no reaction."

	Cornstarch Peanut	Styrofoam Peanut
Solvent		
Acetone		
Saliva		
Water		

2. Look at the illustration below and decide which kind of peanut, styrofoam or cornstarch, would be appropriate for the reaction. Write that name in the box.

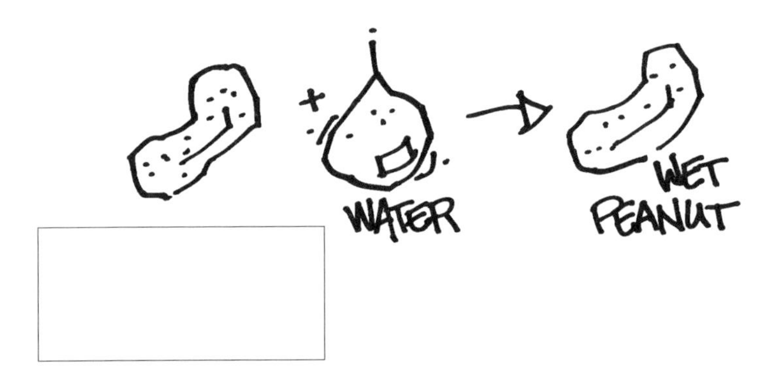

How Come, Huh?

The polystyrene packing peanuts disintegrated in the acetone, just like they did in the previous experiment. But the cornstarch peanuts stayed pretty much the same, until you popped them in your mouth and they dissolved where the polystyrene peanuts wouldn't.

This experiment demonstrates the relationship between the solvent (in this case the water or acetone) and the solvate (the thing you want to try to dissolve, in this case the two kinds of peanuts). If you think of the solvent as a key that has to fit in between the long molecules and unlock them so they can fall apart, you will get an idea of how this works. The acetone does not fit into the spaces of the cornstarch molecules so it cannot unlock them. By the same token, water molecules in your mouth can fit, so the cornstarch peanut dissolves quite easily.

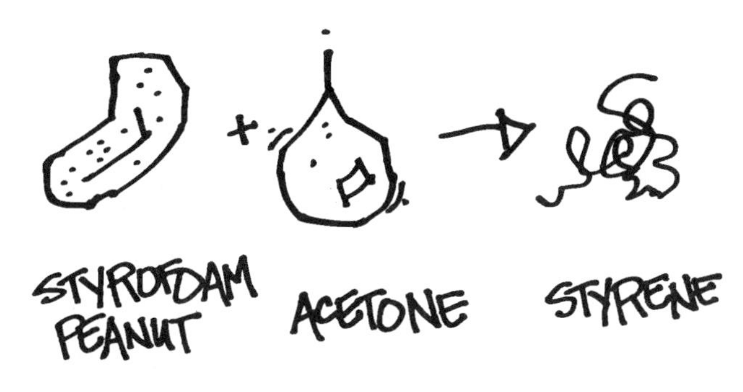

This is a vivid demonstration of a physical change, one that does not change the chemical structure of the participants, they do not recombine or react with one another to form something new—they just change shape.

Science Fair Extensions

50. Try other kinds of plastics. If you check the bottom of most plastic containers, you will find the recycling symbol, three arrows forming a triangle, with a number from 1 to 6 in the center. Test plastics, foams, and gels that have different numbers and see which ones are soluble in acetone.

51. Explore different solvents. If you head to the hardware store, you will find acetone, mineral spirits, paint thinner, turpentine, and a host of other chemicals. Gasoline has been used for years to clean grease off engines and hands. Nab a stack of coffee cups and test each one of these solvents and then see if you can determine why some work while others won't. As always, use good safety techniques, a well-ventilated area, and ASK YOUR PARENTS FIRST!

Big Idea 7

A solution is a mixture of different kinds of matter made up of solvents (liquid) and solutes (molecule-sized solids) that are mixed together evenly. Other kinds of mixtures are emulsions, suspensions, and colloids.

Mixing Oil & Water

The Experiment

First up, emulsions. By definition, an emulsion is a suspended mixture of two or more liquids. The two or more liquids part should not pose any problems in the comprehension department, but suspension just might. When you suspend something as a chemist, it means that you get it to "hang" or stay in place, in solution. Imagine that you blew soap bubbles, and instead of falling to the ground, they just floated in mid-air. You would say that the bubbles are suspended. Same thing with liquids. They are mixed together and instead of falling or rising they just stay where they are—suspended in the mixture.

To create an emulsion we are going to use oil and water to make a mixture that winds up looking like milk. The tricky part is to get the water and oil to like each other, or else they'll separate, and the water will sink to the bottom of the beaker because it's heavier than the cooking oil. To keep the two together, we'll add liquid detergent, which kind of acts like a peacekeeper between the two liquids.

Materials

1 16mm by 150mm Test tube
1 #0, Solid, stopper
1 1 oz. Bottle of cooking oil
1 1 oz. Bottle of liquid detergent
Water

Procedure

1. Fill the test tube one-third full with water. To the water add another third of a tube of cooking oil. The test tube should now be about three-fourths full with a mixture of water and oil. Draw a picture.

Mixing Oil & Water

2. Insert the stopper in the test tube and shake the two liquids vigorously for about 2 minutes. Set the tube down and quickly draw a picture on page 121 of what the contents of the tube look like immediately after they have been shaken.

3. As you draw, continue to observe what is happening to the mixture. After the mixture has had a chance to settle for approximately three minutes, draw a third picture of what you see. Label the individual liquids if you can see them separately.

4. Now, add a dash of liquid detergent to the oil-and-water mixture, stopper, and shake the whole tube again thoroughly for about one minute.

5. After mixing a second time with the detergent added, leave the test tube alone and observe what happens. If the oil and water separate again, you may need to either add more detergent, shake harder, or shake a little longer.

Hopefully, you have created an emulsion—two liquids, oil and water, that both remain suspended in solution after they have been mixed. Draw a picture of what you see in the fourth and final test tube in the Data & Observations section.

6. To clean up all you have to do is rinse the tubes under running water and wipe up any messes that may have been created.

Data & Observations

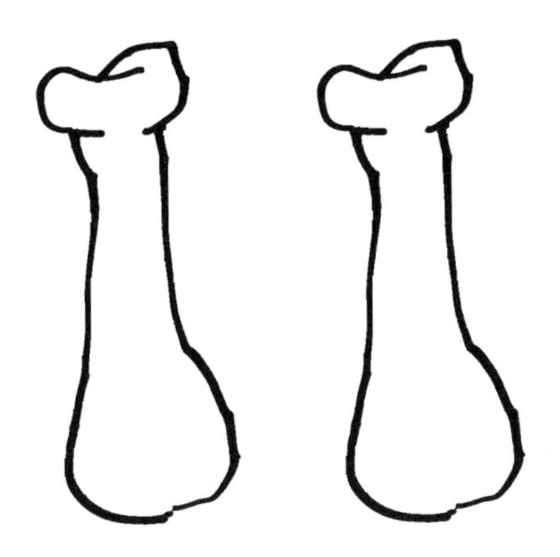

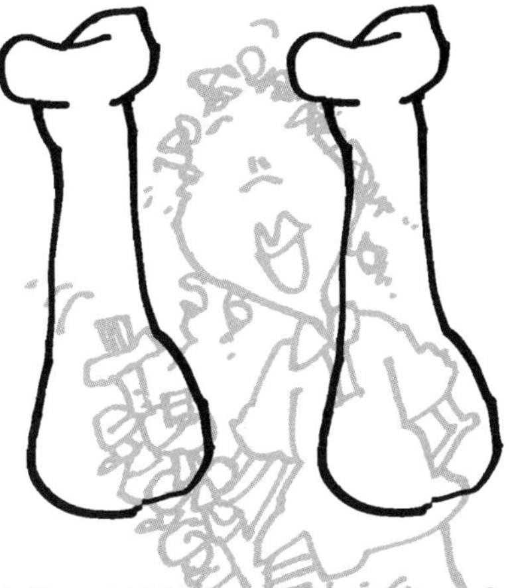

Oil and Water No Mixing | *Oil and Water After Mixing* | *Oil and Water After Settling* | *Oil, Water, Soap After Mixing*

How Come, Huh?

When mixing oil and water, the oil will break up into small droplets and be dispersed in the water very temporarily. After leaving the test tube with the mixture alone for a while, the two clear liquids will separate, with the oil forming a layer above the water because of its lighter density and generally more snobby nature. After adding some liquid detergent (also known by the fancy chemistry words *the emulsifier*) and doing some vigorous shaking, the small droplets of oil will stay dispersed forming an emulsion, or a suspended mixture of two or more liquids.

Just for kitchen chemistry type of reference, other examples of common emulsions that you will probably find in your house are milk (cow fat and water), mayonnaise (fat and water), salad dressings (oil and vinegar), and butter (cream and cow tails).

Science Fair Extensions

52. Emulsions are used in cooking all the time. Do a little research and find out some common emulsions besides mayonnaise.

Mutant Milk Maggots

The Experiment

Nothing like a cold glass of . . . mutant milk maggots to satisfy your thirst. OK, they're not really mutant maggots, just regular old microbes that accidentally fell off the udders of the cow. Nope? OK, it's curdled milk.

Materials

1 Toobe or other container
1 1 oz. Bottle of acetic acid
1 4 oz. Serving of warm, whole milk

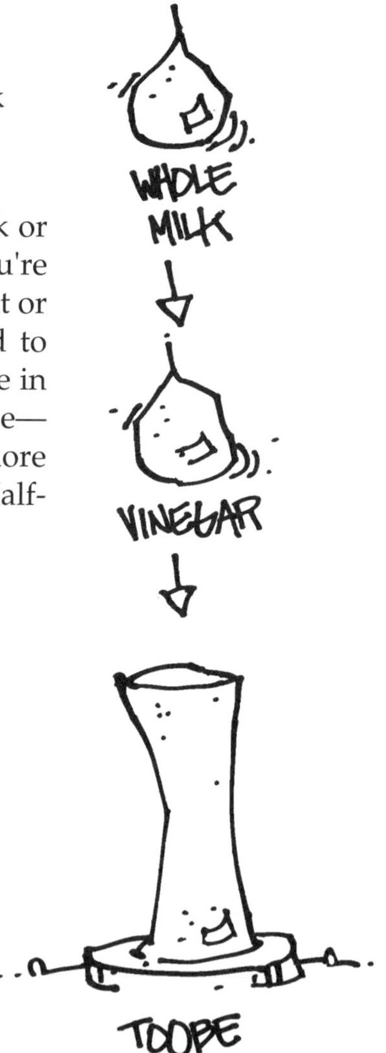

Procedure

1. Add the 4 oz. of warm, whole milk or cream to the Toobe or other container. If you're trying to be chintzy and get by with 2 percent or skim milk instead of whole milk, you need to know that the more fat and protein you have in the milk, the plumper your maggots will be—everyone knows fat maggots are much more likely to be found in whole milk or cream. Half-and-half is also a good hideout.

2. Add 1 oz. of acetic acid—this is household vinegar—to the milk and let it stand undisturbed for about 2 minutes, but keep an eye on the glass.

3. The maggots will start to appear in just a couple of seconds; you'll be able to see them swimming around in the glass. They usually surface near the top half of the Toobe—they are cream in color and are about the size of a pinhead.

Data & Observations

Draw a picture of the milk suspension before the vinegar was added and after.

Before

After

How Come, Huh?

Milk is actually a suspension. It contains molecules of protein and fat that are so small that they cannot be seen by the naked eye.

Cream-colored lumps of curdled fat and protein will begin to form almost immediately. Because these lumps are heavier than the liquid, they will eventually fall to the bottom of the glass. When this happens, you will have successfully separated the white, solid, milk particles from the clearer liquid.

Mutant Milk Maggots

Milk is a colloid. There's that word again. A colloid is a mixture of two different things: In this case, solids mixed into a liquid. In milk, the solid molecules of protein and fat are so little and spread out so evenly that they seem to be invisible. But, when you add the vinegar, which is a weak acid, it causes these fat and protein molecules to scrunch up and hook on to one another, forming lumps in the milk.

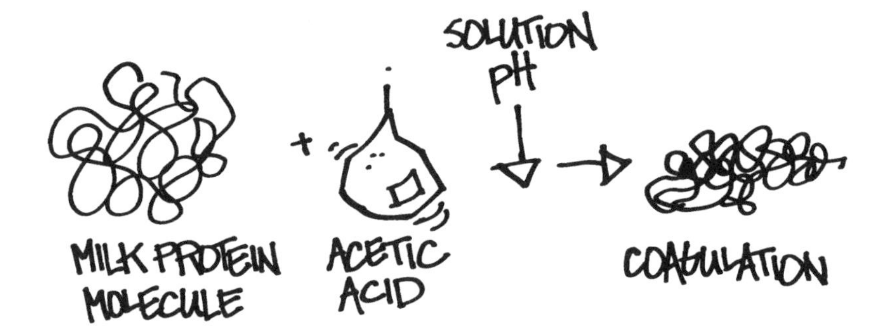

The *solid* lumps of fat and protein are called the *curd* and the *liquid* portion is the *whey*. So now when you read that children's rhyme about little Miss Muffet and her curds and whey, you'll know she was actually doing a science experiment and not just fiddling around having a snack.

Science Fair Extensions

53. Temperature is always a big factor when it comes to chemical reactions. This experiment should fall into line. Repeat the lab activity using milk of different temperatures.

54. The fat content of the milk may also have something to do with this lab. Try nonfat, 1 percent, 2 percent, whole, half-and-half, and cream. Compare the number and size of milk maggots that are formed when the vinegar is added.

Elmer's Bouncing Blob

The Experiment

Ordinary white glue is going to be added to ordinary borax to make an extraordinary batch of glue glop that you can bounce, press on to paper, and hang from your ear—not necessarily in that order. In addition to that, you are going to complete the grand slam of solutions and compose your very own colloid. This is how it is done.

White glue is a liquid. Borax can be added to water to make a liquid officially known as sodium tetraborate. When these two liquids are mixed with one another, they hook together but do not form a new compound.

Think of a pickup truck and a boat. You can back the truck up and hook on to the boat trailer. They form one unit, but they are still two separate vehicles and can be separated again at a later date. Glue and borax are the same way chemically. They will hook together and form a longer chain, but they are still borax and glue. We call this kind of a reaction a colloid.

Materials

1 1 oz. Bottle of glue solution
1 1 oz. Bottle of 2% sodium tetraborate solution
1 1 mL Pipette
1 5 oz. Wax cup
1 Plastic, sealable baggie
1 Craft stick
1 Bottle food coloring

Elmer's Bouncing Blob

Procedure

1. Shake the glue solution for 20 seconds before you open the bottle because this stuff settles when it sits around. Pour the entire contents of the bottle of glue into the wax cup.

2. Using the pipette add 2 milliliters of sodium tetraborate to the glue solution, and using the craft stick, stir with reckless abandon until a blob starts to form. This usually takes 15–20 seconds.

3. When most of the liquid has turned into a rubbery blob that is clinging to the craft stick, pull the whole mess out of the cup and peel it off into your fingers. Roll the ball of glue glop around in your hand. This will help to dry out the colloid.

4. Time to experiment. Try bouncing the glop on the table. Find an old newspaper and make an impression of the text or pictures by pressing the blob onto the paper. Let it hang and stretch from your fingers. Have fun.

5. When you are done, put it in a sealable plastic bag so it won't dry out. If you are not a hoarder or saver, you can toss the glop into the garbage without fear of contaminating the world's water supply after this lab activity is over.

Data & Observations

1. Describe the texture of a glue/borax colloid. ____.

2. List 4 words that describe what you can do with your colloid.
   a. Bounce

   b. ____________________
   c. ____________________
   d. ____________________
   e. ____________________

How Come, Huh?

White glue is made up of long molecules. Just like the analogy of the truck and the boat trailer, the sodium tetraborate hooks all of these long glue molecules together, forming a tangled web of molecules trapped in water. The water gives the colloid the character of being a liquid.

Science Fair Extensions

55. Compare your colloid with the commercial product, Silly Putty™. List the similarities and differences of the two compounds.

56. Experiment with different brands of white glue as well as different brands of borax. Compare your results.

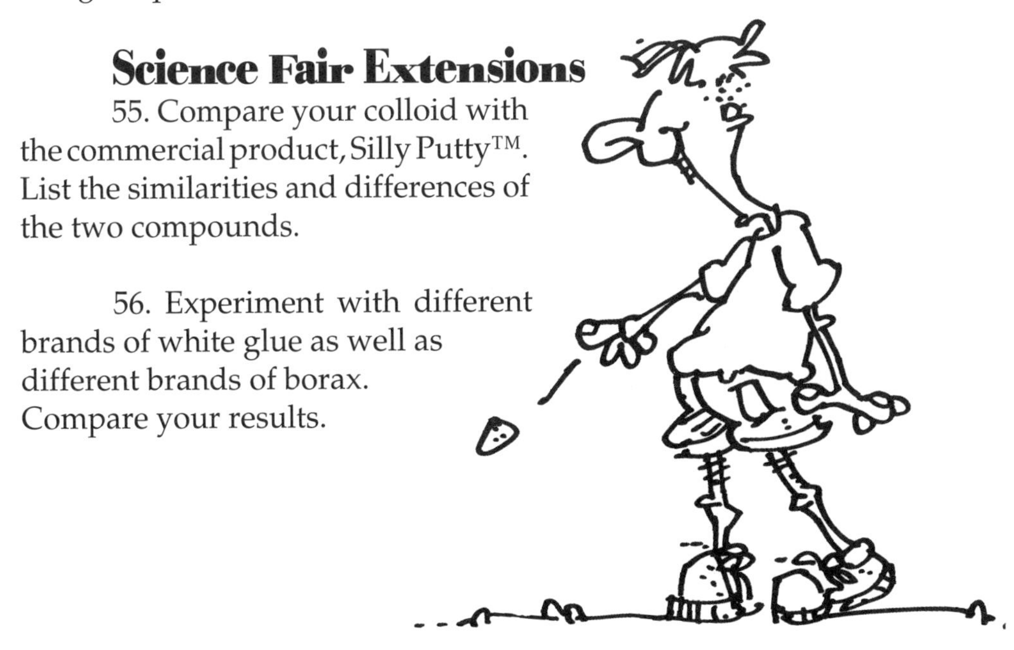

Big Idea 8

Once new compounds form, the elements tend to remain connected together. Mixtures, on the other hand, are made up of different kinds of matter that can be separated from one another using filters, crystallization, evaporation, or even magnets.

Muddy Waters

The Experiment

When two or more chemicals come in contact with one another and hook together to form a new compound, it is just exactly that—a new compound. It will have a new boiling point, freezing point, and a new density. The color may have changed, an odor may now be produced. There are definite and discernible changes.

A mixture, on the other hand, is like a big party. Everyone comes together and mingles around, but they separate and go home at the end of the night. The separating of chemicals can be done in a variety of ways—filtering, precipitation, crystallization, and even using magnets. This first lab uses a process that is common to chemists—filtration.

Materials

3 2 -Liter pop bottles, with caps, empty
2 Filter papers or paper towels
Water
Mud, lint, dirt, sand, paper punches, et cetera

Procedure

1. Place all of the mud, dirt, lint, and et cetera into the 2 -liter pop bottle. Add water until it is almost full.

2. Shake the bottle until the mud, dirt, lint, and gook is stirred up into a nice, cloudy, mixture. Examine the contents of the bottle, and you will see that a lot of the heavy stuff has settled but that the finer things are still racing around in the top half of the bottle.

Muddy Waters

3. Now that you have a mess on your hands insert a piece of filter paper or paper napkin folded into a cone shape into the neck of a second clean pop bottle.

Gently pour the contents of the first bottle into the filter paper and watch what happens to the mud, sand, and gook.

4. Pour the entire contents of the first bottle into the second bottle. Insert a filter paper in to the neck of the third bottle and pour the once-filtered contents of the second bottle into the third—filtering them a third time.

5. When you are done filtering, place the papers in an area where they can dry and you can successfully demonstrate that you can separate a mixture by using a filter.

How Come, Huh?

The particles suspended in the water were bigger than the pores in the paper so when you poured the contents of the bottle into the paper the water molecules zipped on through, but the mud, dirt, sand, and other assorted gook got caught. Voila, you have separation.

Science Fair Extensions

57. When you do the experiment Ironing Out Sand on page 134, incorporate the use of filters to separate the sand and the salt water.

Snowstorm in a Tube

The Experiment

This reaction produces crystals by precipitation. This word may conjure up images of rain or snow, but it also applies to crystal growth. Rain is produced when water droplets start to form on particles of dust in the air. As more and more molecules of water jump on the dust particle, the drop of water becomes heavier. When it finally gets too heavy for the cloud to hang onto, it drops to the ground.

In this experiment, two chemicals are mixed together. The alcohol causes the potassium sulfate molecules to start to clump together, forming crystals. When the crystals get too heavy to be supported by the liquid in the tube, they fall—or crash, to use chemists' terms—out of solution. It will be like having your own personal snowstorm, only you won't have to shovel the driveway.

Materials

1 Pair of goggles
1 16 mm x 150 mm Test tube
1 1 oz. Bottle of potassium sulfate solution (10% solution)
1 1 oz. Bottle of isopropyl alcohol (70%)
1 1 mL Pipette
1 Hand lens
1 Pencil

Snowstorm in a Tube

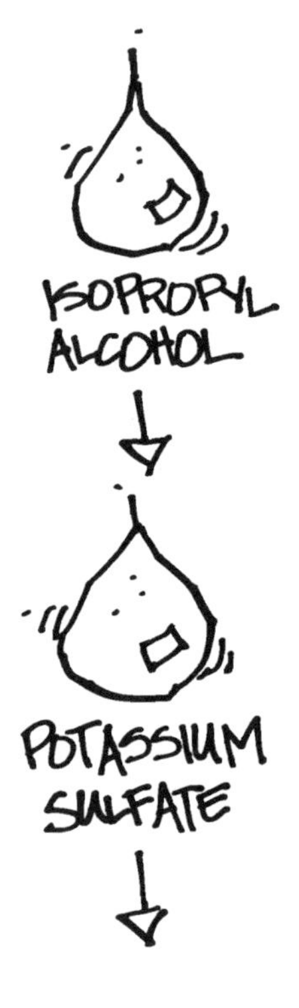

Procedure

1. Goggle up. Fill the test tube about two-thirds of the way full with 10% potassium sulfate solution.

2. Open the bottle of isopropyl alcohol, squeeze the bulb of the pipette and fill it by releasing the bulb. Slowly add 10 drops of alcohol to the test tube that has the potassium sulfate in it. You will immediately notice that a cloudy layer appears at the top of the tube. These are crystals starting to form.

3. Add a couple more drops of isopropyl alcohol to increase the snowstorm. At this point, take your hand lens and examine the crystals as they start to fall toward the bottom of the tube. The entire reaction takes about five minutes to complete, so hang in there.

4. You can pour everything down the drain when you are finished.

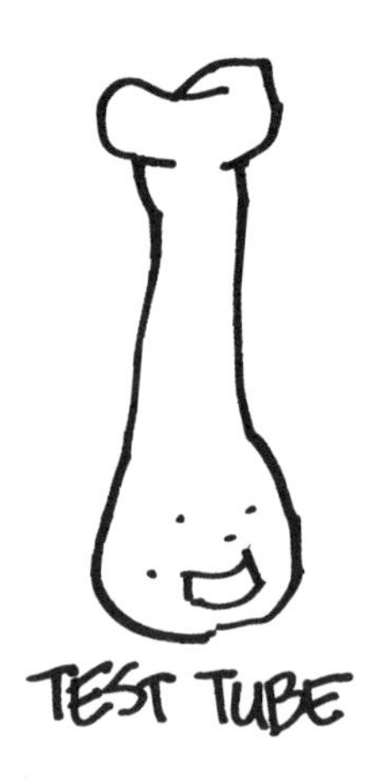

Data & Observations

Describe what you saw in the space provided below.

____

____

____

____

____

How Come, Huh?

Basically the rubbing alcohol and the potassium sulfate do not like each other. So, when you add drops of rubbing alcohol into the solution, it causes the potassium sulfate to crash. In other words, the rubbing alcohol causes the molecules of potassium sulfate to clump together and form big crystals that we can see with the naked eye.

As these crystals get bigger and bigger, they start to weigh too much for the water in the solution to support so they fall very slowly to the bottom of the tube. Just like in the weather, this is called precipitation. Another term for this is "crashing out of solution," and it is one of the ways that we can separate mixture and solutions.

Science Fair Extensions

58. You were using a 10% solution to study the effect of isopropyl alcohol on that solution. Experiment with different concentrations and see if the size of the crystals is influenced.

59. Temperature creates all sorts of problems and solutions for chemists. Generally, the warmer a reaction is, the faster it takes place. Repeat this experiment, but try heating the potassium sulfate and then the isopropyl alcohol to see if the increased temperature makes a difference.

60. Try the experiment again, only cool the chemicals this time. Are the crystal sizes smaller, do they form at a slower rate? What's going on here?

Ironing Out Sand

The Experiment

Chemicals compounds have lots of different kinds of characteristics, and these characteristics are used by chemists to separate and identify different compounds. They are also the basis for organizing the chemicals into the Table of the Elements.

In this lab we are going to take advantage of three different ways that these chemicals can be separated from one another—magnetism, solubility, and insolubility—and use them to separate a mixture.

Materials

1 5" Pie tin
1 1 oz. Bottle of sand
1 1 oz. Bottle of iron filings
1 1 oz. Bottle of sodium chloride
1 Craft stick
1 Test tube
1 Stopper
1 Magnet
1 Napkin
1 5-oz. Wax cup
Water

Procedure

1. Place the pie tin in the middle of your lab area and add a half a cap of sand to the pan. Next add a half a cap of iron filings, and finally a half a cap of sand. Pour all of the ingredients into the test tube, stopper, and shake. Pour them back out into the pan.

2. You should have a uniform mixture of iron, sand, and salt. If this were ever of any use to anyone it would be great, but unfortunately this combination of compounds is good for only one thing that we know of—this lab.

3. Wrap the magnet in the napkin and run it through the mixture. Neither sand or salt are attracted to magnets, which means that the only thing that the magnet should remove from the mixture are the iron filings. One, down, one to do.

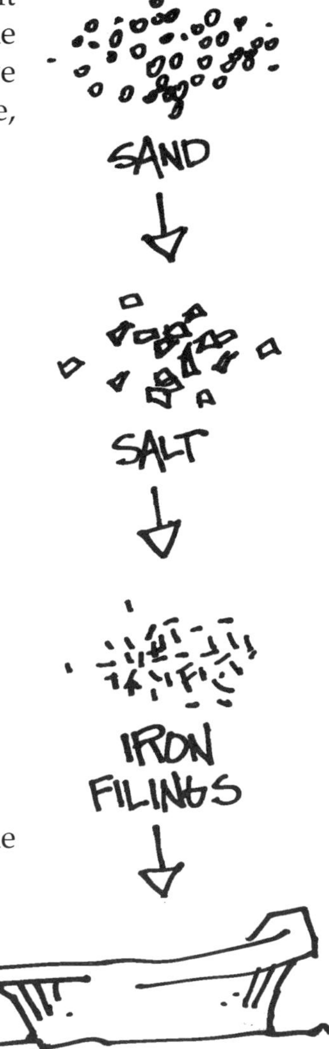

4. Place the sand and salt mixture in the 5-oz. wax cup and fill the cup half full of water. The salt will dissolve, the sand will not. Pour the salt water into the pie tin. Set it aside and allow it to evaporate.

Ironing Out Sand

5. The salt will appear on the pie tin as a crystal, and the sand will remain in the bottom of the cup and eventually dry out. All three compounds have been separated from the mixture.

How Come, Huh?

Each of the three different compounds is composed of different atoms that are arranged in different shapes that all lead to different characteristics.

The iron filings, like all iron objects, have a magnetic pole field surrounding them that is produced by a north and south pole. This magnetic field is attracted to other magnetic fields and allows you to separate out that one compound.

Salt is composed of sodium chloride, and sand is made out of primarily silicon and oxygen. The characteristics of salt permit it to dissolve in water, where the characteristics of sand do not allow it to dissolve.

Science Fair Extensions

61. Create your own mixtures and test them in your lab. We use caffeine, which can be sublimated, and sodium bicarbonate, which can be dissolved out using acetic acid in other mixtures that we have created for this same purpose. Try separating these two mixtures:

1. Caffeine, sand, and iron filings
2. Baking soda, caffeine, and sand
3. Sand, salt, caffeine, with a couple of iron filings for flavor

Salt Crust Pan

The Experiment

When salt is dissolved in water, you have created a mixture. The salt dissolves into atom-size particles that are suspended in the solvent, which, in this case, is the water. One way to separate this mixture back into its components is to use the process of evaporation to produce crystals.

Materials

1 Water, hot, 1 cup
1 Spoon , plastic
1 Salt, 1/2 cup
1 5" Tart pan

Procedure

1. Slowly pour the salt into the cup of hot water, stirring it with the spoon until it all dissolves. Let it sit for a few minutes, then stir again.

2. Let the salt water sit for another minute to settle, then pour it into the tart pan. If there is salt in the bottom of the cup that has not dissolved, pour it into the bottom of the tart pan as well. It will not have any effect on the outcome of the experiment.

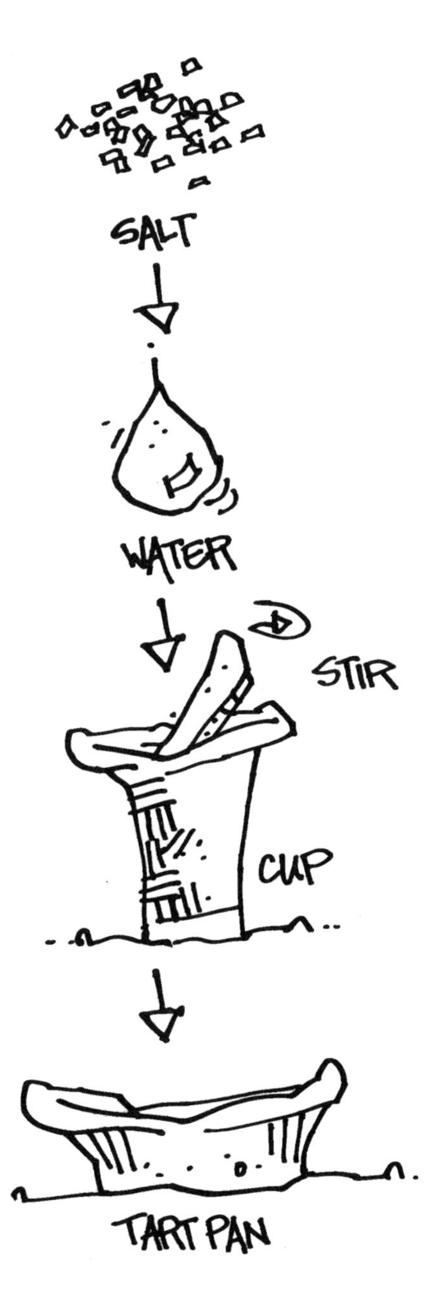

Salt Crust Pan

3. Place the tart pan in an open area until all of the water has evaporated. As the water evaporates, it leaves the dissolved salt behind, forming the crystals you see. Depending on the conditions, you may have nice large crystals or many small granular crystals.

How Come, Huh?

When you stir the salt into the water, the crystals dissolve into small molecule-sized pieces and float in the water.

In almost any environment, water that is left exposed to the air will eventually evaporate. When it does, it separates itself from the other impurities in the solution, leaving them behind. In this case, the salt crystals are the impurities and as they find themselves being abandoned, they hook on to one another and form a group called a crystal.

The more water that evaporates, the more salt molecules cling together. If the process is slow, then more salt molecules have time to find one another and bigger crystals result. If the process is quick, then the crystals are small. This is true of all conditions whether in the chemistry lab or outdoors during the formation of rocks and minerals.

Science Fair Extensions

62. Repeat the experiment using other salts like potassium sulfate, copper sulfate, nickel sulfate, sodium sulfate, calcium chloride, or other compounds like sugar.

63. Experiment with the rate of cooling and the size of crystals that are produced during the reaction.

Creepy Colors

The Experiment

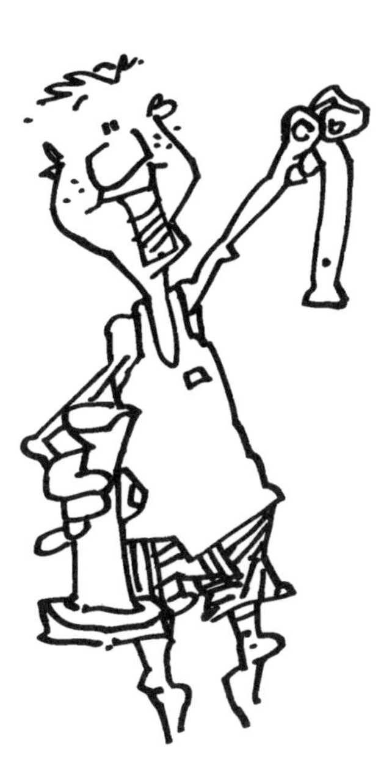

Black ink is not black. Silly as that may sound at first it's true. Black inks have all sorts of colors hidden in them. Sometimes as many as six separate and distinct colors can be separated out and identified.

One of the processes that allows you to separate out these colors is called chromatography. *Chroma* translates to color, and a *graph* is a picture. So chromatography is a color picture of the mixture of ink that you placed on the paper.

Materials

1 Toobe or other container
  Water
1 12" strip of paper
1 Black, water-soluble, felt-tipped pen
1 Craft stick
1 Strip of tape

Procedure

1. Add an inch of water to the bottom of the Toobe.

2. Cut a long, slender piece of paper that is three-fourths inch wide and 12 inches long. Using the water-soluble, felt-tipped pen, make a thick, black dot 1 1/2 inches up from the bottom of the paper, just like the illustration on page 140.

3. Lower the paper so that it just touches the bottom of the Toobe but make sure that the dot of black ink does not get in the water. If it looks like the dot is going to get wet, pull the paper out of the Toobe, empty a bit of water out, and lower the paper into the Toobe again.

Creepy Colors

4. Place the craft stick on top of the Toobe and tape the paper to it so that it holds it in place. Set the Toobe in an area where it will remain undisturbed.

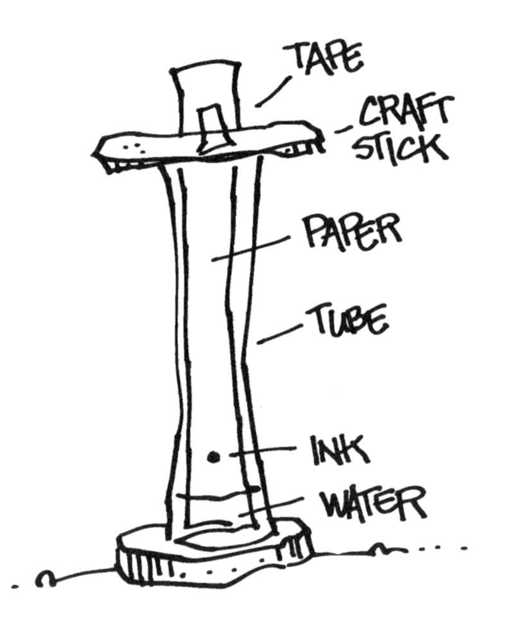

Data & Observations

Make observations every hour for as long as possible. After 24 hours, your separation will be complete. Either cut and tape your separation to the space provided to the right, or using colored pencils, copy the separation as accurately as you can.

How Come, Huh?

The separation of pigments using this technique is called paper chromatography. As the water travels up the paper, it dissolves the ink and literally picks it up and starts to carry the different colors with it. Every color migrates at different speeds and different distances, this is due to the difference in shape and weight. As the water travels up the paper, the heavier inks get left behind and dry in place; the light, easier-to-transport inks zip along with the water.

Science Fair Extensions

64. Try different brands of inks and see which colors they use to make the black color that you see on the page.

65. Try this same experiment with different solvents. Check with an adult first, but things like acetone, rubbing alcohol, soda pop, and other household items could be tested for results.

66. If you really want to get fancy, you can not only check the colors of inks but also the different pigments and colors of compounds found in the leaves and flowers of a variety of plants. Collect the leaves of the plant you want to test, cut them into small pieces with a pair of scissors, and put them in a coffee cup. Add a little bit of acetone and continue to mash the leaves with the butt of a screwdriver handle or other blunt object. When you have a greenish paste, dab a small drop of it on the paper where you would normally put the drop of ink. Put a small amount of acetone in your Toobe and place this in a well-ventilated area.

Big Idea 9

Solids, liquids, and gases can diffuse into liquids and gases. The rate they diffuse is affected by temperature, pressure, and concentration.

Slow-Motion Rainbow

The Experiment

There are actually two parts to this lab activity. The first is to experiment with a chemical that has the ability to absorb very large quantities of water. You will record this ability by drawing the outline of the crystal as it grows.

The second part of the lab will be to observe the mixing of colors as drops of food coloring migrate—actually diffuse would be the appropriate word—through these same crystals and produce new colors as they mix with one another very slowly.

Materials

1 Vial of polyacrylamide crystals
1 Pre-form tube
1 4 oz. Cup with warm water
1 Box of food colors
1 Clock with sweep second hand
1 Metric ruler

Procedure

1. Open the bottle of polyacrylamide crystals (ghost crystals) and pour a small pile out on to the table. Select one, nice, large crystal from the assortment. Place that crystal in the box labeled "0 minutes" on page 145 and trace the outline of the crystal in the center of the box. Fill the cup full of warm water and drop the crystal into it; let it soak for 5 minutes.

2. While you are waiting to measure the increase in size of the crystal in the cup, place 20 to 25 crystals in the bottom of the Pre-form tube. Fill the tube with warm water and set it aside.

Slow-Motion Rainbow

3. When the 5 minutes has passed, take the crystal out of the water, place it in the second box on page 145 and trace the outline. Measure the diameter of the crystal and record that measurement in the space provided

4. Repeat this portion of the experiment two more times, allowing the crystal to soak in the warm water for 5 minutes, then removing the crystal and measuring the increase in size. When you are done with this crystal, place it in the Pre-form tube with the other crystals.

5. Let the crystals sit for 15 minutes while they absorb water and plump up a bit. When they look like small, clear, ice-cube marshmallows, you are ready for the next step.

6. Cover the tube with your hand so that you do not lose any of the crystals and pour the excess water from the tube down the drain.

7. Add a drop of yellow, red, and blue food coloring to the crystals in the top of the tube. The food coloring will slowly start to dissolve into the solid, liquid mash that you have created. Using the spaces provided on page 145 to record the colors that you see at 0 minutes, 5 minutes, 10 minutes, and 15 minutes into the experiment.

WATER

GHOST CRYSTALS

Data & Observations

Use the spaces on the following page to record the size of the crystals and the colors that are produced.

Data & Observations

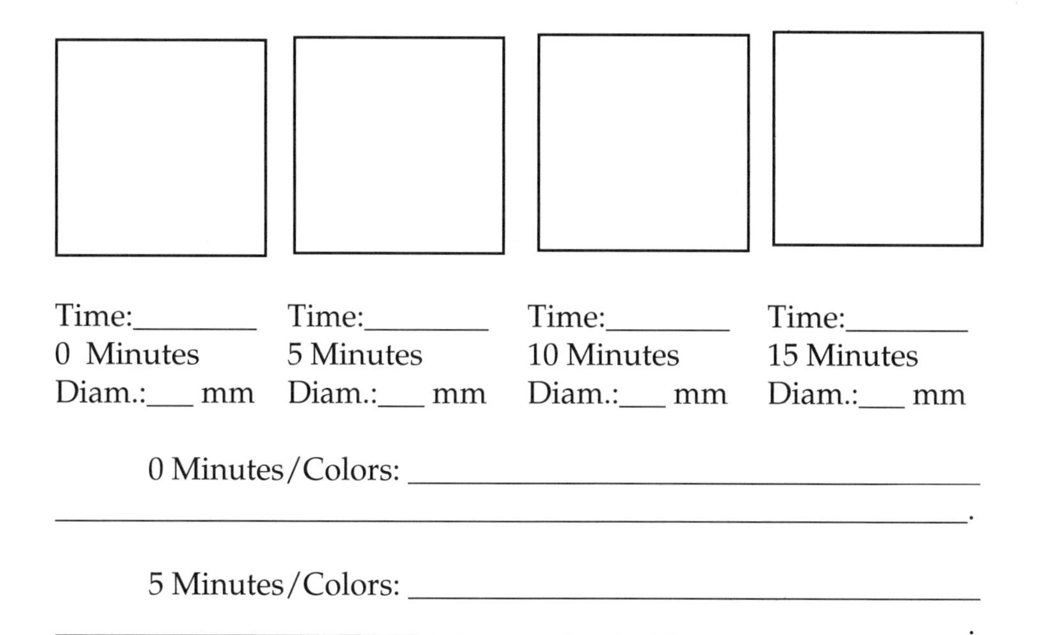

Time:_______	Time:_______	Time:_______	Time:_______
0 Minutes	5 Minutes	10 Minutes	15 Minutes
Diam.:___ mm	Diam.:___ mm	Diam.:___ mm	Diam.:___ mm

0 Minutes/Colors: ______________________________
____.

5 Minutes/Colors: ______________________________
____.

10 Minutes/Colors_______
____
________________________.
________________________.

How Come, Huh?

The dehydrated crystals are actually made of a highly absorbent polymer called anioic polyacrylamide. This compound can absorb upwards of 500 times its weight in water. As the ink diffuses through the liquid/solid mash, it slowly spreads out taking up a much greater suface area.

Thermal Ink Clouds

The Experiment

Rumor has it that the temperature of a liquid will directly affect the speed that a dye or drop of food coloring in that liquid will diffuse or spread out.

Since we believe this statement to be largely accurate, we are going to help you set up an experiment to demonstrate this very idea using two Toobes—one full of hot water and the other cold—and a little food coloring.

Materials

2 Toobes or other containers
1 Bottle of food coloring
Water, cold
Water, hot

Procedure

1. Fill one Toobe or other container with very hot water and the other Toobe with very cold water.

2. Place one drop of food coloring in each of the respective Toobes at as nearly the same time as is possible.

3. Observe the movement of the food coloring every minute. Record the perimeters of the ink drops as they expand, using a dotted line, in the spaces provided below.

Data & Observations

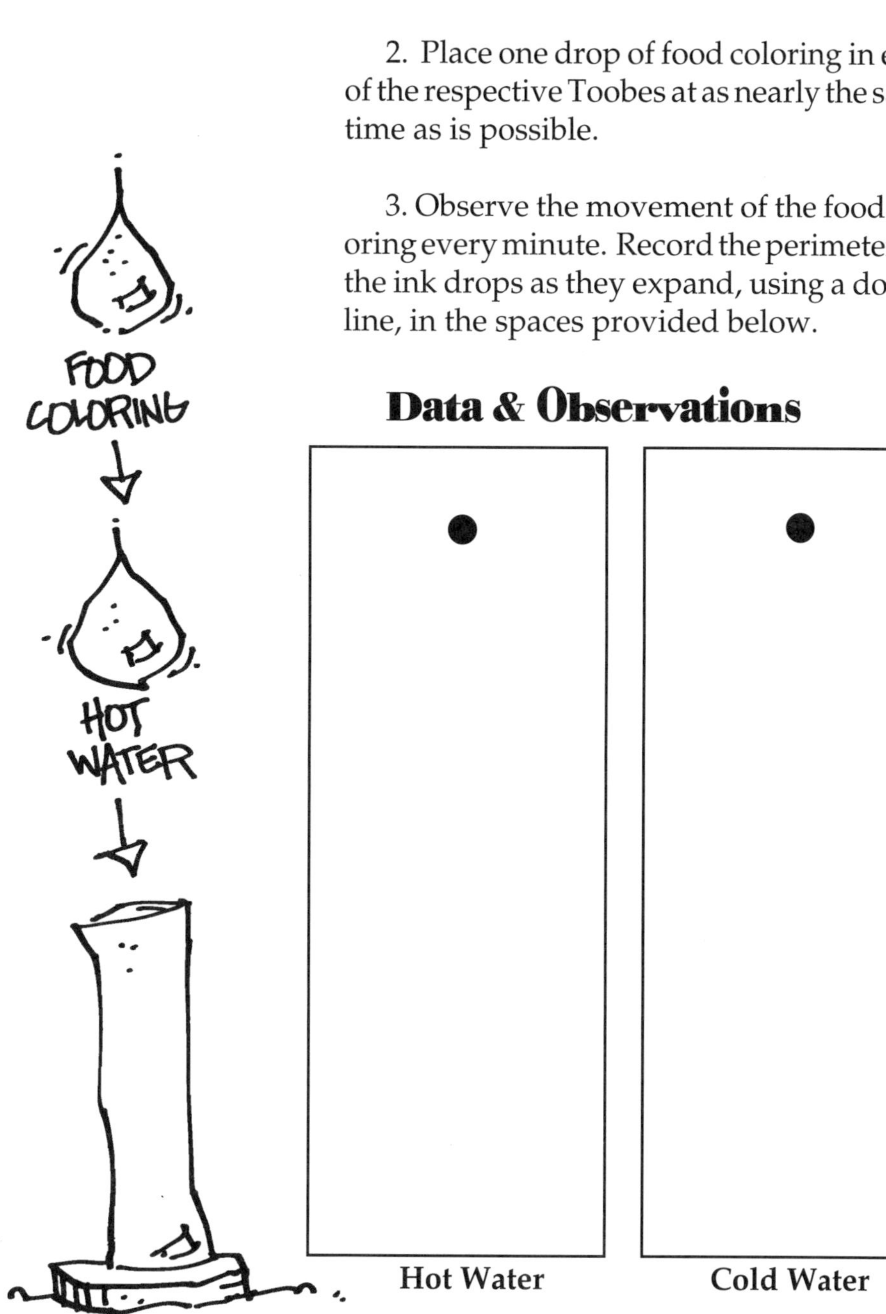

Thermal Ink Clouds

How Come, Huh?

In the first part of the experiment, the food coloring is heavier than the water, so it diffuses down into it over time. The second part of the experiment has to do with the density of liquids when they are heated. As water molecules are heated, they bump around more, need to spread out, and as a consequence, take up more room. A chemist would say that the liquid became less dense, or the same number of molecules took up more space. Think of a sack of marbles. When all of the marbles are in the sack, they are crammed very close together. They are very dense. If you empty them out on to the floor, they spread out. Same number of marbles, just taking up more room—less dense.

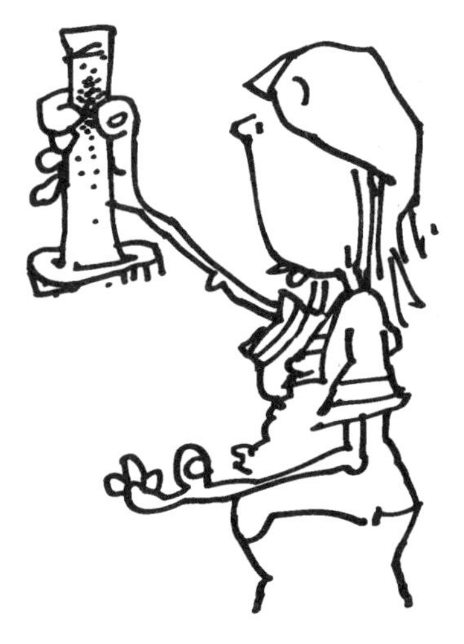

Warmer liquids that are less dense tend to rise if they are surrounded by colder liquids. This is called a convection current. In this case the warm water in the bottle was less dense than the cold water in the Toobe so it migrated to the top.

Science Fair Extensions

67. Design an experiment to demonstrate that the greater the difference in temperature between the warm water in the bottle and the cold water in the Toobe, the faster the water rises to the top.

68. Change the shape of the warm water container and see if the experiment is altered in any way.

69. Try this same experiment with different liquids.

Mixing Colors

The Experiment

We are going to take advantage of a change in environment, specifically the pH of a solution, to create pressure inside a solution that will then produce a variety of colors from the three primary colors. Whole milk contains fats and proteins that are very sensitive to changes in pH. If the pH is raised or lowered, even just a bit, it causes these long molecules to bend, wiggle, and fold around one another causing movement or pressure on the concentrated ink. This pressure mixes the food coloring you added to the milk.

Materials

1 9"-12" Pie tin
1 Pint of whole milk, warm
1 Bottle of red food coloring
1 Bottle of blue food coloring
1 Bottle of yellow food coloring
1 Bottle of liquid soap
1 Box of crayons

Procedure

1. Fill the pie tin with warm, whole milk. Cream or half-and-half also works very well—the more fat the better.

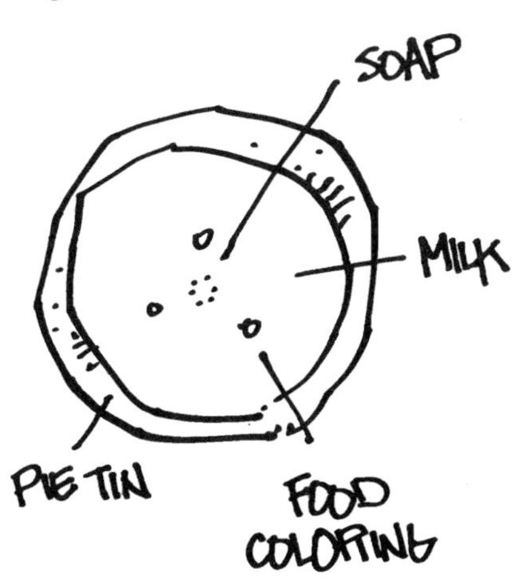

Mixing Colors

2. Using the three primary colors of food coloring create a small equilateral triangle, 1" on a side, in the center of the milk. Using two drops of each food coloring works well. Observe the movement of the food coloring for about 60 seconds.

3. Add a drop of liquid soap to the very center of the triangle. You should immediately notice the effect the soap has on the proteins and fats in the milk.

4. Once the reaction starts to slow down, add drops of soap to different areas around the pie tin and the reaction will start up again.

How Come, Huh?

Protein and fat molecules are very long and complex. They have several kinds of bonds, or connections, holding them together. When you added the liquid soap, you raised the pH of the milk, and the soap started stealing the hydrogen atoms from these long molecules. This caused the proteins and fats to collapse and curl up into large clumps. Consequently, this collapsing bumped the food-coloring molecules and mixed them with one another.

Draw a picture of the colors you see in the pie tin after five minutes of mixing and then after ten minutes.

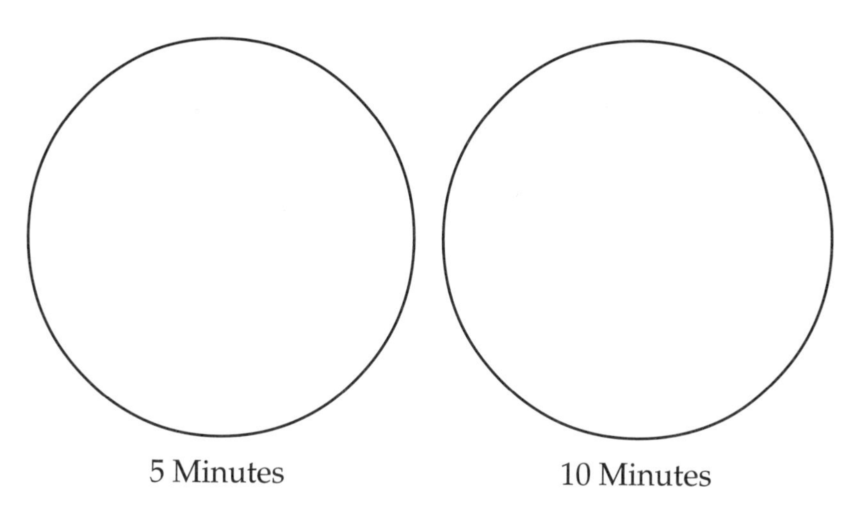

Science Fair Extensions

70. Repeat the experiment and use a variety of different milks: nonfat, 1 percent, 2 percent, whole, and cream. Keep the temperature the same and record the difference in the way the colors are produced.

71. Repeat the experiment but change the temperature of the milk and see if that has any effect on the rate the colors are mixed.

72. Repeat the reaction with other bases (ammonia, bleach, etc.) and acids (lemon juice, vinegar). Determine if pH of the additive is a factor based on your observations.

Dehydrated Grape Dance

The Experiment

Gases can be dissolved into liquids and that particular fact is experienced by some folks on a near daily basis. Carbon dioxide is the gas that is dissolved into soda pop liquid to give it the bubbly, fizzy appearance that you see when you pop the top off a bottle or can.

This lab also doubles as a lab on density. As the carbon dioxide adheres to the sides of raisins that are placed in the soft drink, they become buoyant and rise to the surface of the container. If they lose their carbon dioxide floats any time along the way, they become heavy and fall to the bottom again.

And finally, if you really want to have some fun, you can make up a story about sewer maggots, and totally gross out your friends. Inquiring minds want to know, and we will tell all.

Materials

1 Can of Mountain Dew™
1 Toobe or other container
1 Box of raisins in a plastic tub
1 Cup of water, warm

Procedure

1. Open the can of Mountain Dew™ and pour it into the glass. Mountain Dew™, by design, is a yellowish liquid that could be easily presented as a sample of recently acquired sewer water. This is not to say that it tastes or in any other way resembles sewer water, lest the legal counsel for Pepsi Co. sees a potential legal suit on the horizon.

2. Announce to your friends that you have a sample of sewer water, and that you want to introduce them to the insect community via a little critter called a sewer maggot. The sewer maggot, you explain, is used to purify the water. When sewer maggots are added to the sewer water, they can be seen diving up and down, gulping the various nutrients available. Drop about 10 to 15 raisins, which have been soaking in warm water for about a half an hour, into the Mountain Dew™ and they will start to bob up and down.

3. If you want to play this out a little bit more, you can explain that the sewer maggots swim around in the "pee" water and make it potable—a fancy word that means that you can drink it. To prove this to your friends take the container of "pee" water and sip it. Mmmm, mmmm, good. A little salty but good.

4. If they are not on the verge of tossing chunks yet, you can put them there by also telling them that maggots or larvae are a rich source of protein and considered delicacies in some areas of the world. Again, to prove this to them, catch a sewer maggot and pop it in your mouth.

How Come, Huh?

This is more physics than it is chemistry. The bubbles of carbon dioxide stick to the sides of the raisins. When they do this, they decrease the average density of the raisin—the gas makes them less dense than the soda pop—and they float to the top of the Toobe.

Dehydrated Grape Dance

When the raisins get to the top, they start to roll and some of the gas is released. This makes the overall weight of the raisin heavier, and it starts to fall to the bottom of the container.

Science Fair Extensions

73. The fizz that is present in all soda pop is called carbonation. The reason it has this name is that carbon dioxide—carbonic gas—is dissolved into the pop. Try the previous experiment with soda pop that has been sitting out for several hours and has had a chance to de-gas.

74. When you soaked the raisins in the warm water, they plumped up significantly and floated to the surface of the container quickly. Design an experiment where you try this procedure using raisins that have been soaked for different amounts of time in water and raisins that have been dehydrated even more by placing them in an oven. See which kind works best and determine why.

75. Experiment with different kinds of soda and see if one is better than the others for dissolved gas content.

76. Change the item that is floating. Instead of raisins that have been soaked in water try pieces of spaghetti, pieces of pasta, let your imagination run wild and then chase it down. However, NEVER EAT ANYTHING THAT DOES NOT START OUT AS A FOOD PRODUCT TO BEGIN WITH.

Big Idea 10

Water is a bipolar molecule made up of two positively charged hydrogen atoms and one negatively charged oxygen atom. Creating a mini-magnet. The attraction between two water molecules is responsible for things like surface tension, capillary action, and cohesion.

Water Slide

The Experiment

Water molecules are incredibly good at hanging on to one another. The reason for this is that it is a bipolar molecule. Fancy word? Maybe, but easy to understand. *Bi* means two, and *polar* refers to the poles or ends of a magnet where the magnetic field is strongest. So a water molecule is actually a little magnet with a positive end and negative end. Put two or more in a container and they are attracted to one another.

This arrangement gives water some unique characteristics that produce effects like surface tension, capillary action, and cohesion—all of which will be demonstrated in the next 10 lab activities.

We are going to start with cohesion—a term that could be defined as "sticky." You are going to fill a clean, empty soup can with water and pour that water, along a cotton string, down to another soup can without spilling any water.

Materials

2 #303 Soup cans
1 Cotton string, 18" length
Water

Procedure

1. Fill the soup can with water. Dip the entire piece of cotton string into the water and get it soaking wet.

2. Using the illustration on the bottom of the previous page, stretch the string from one can to the other. Make sure the ends are inside the cans.

3. Hold the can full of water higher than the empty can and keeping the ends of the strings in place with your fingers, tip the can just a bit to start a stream of water trickling down the string. As the can empties, tip it just a bit more and the water will continue to flow until you have emptied the top can and filled the bottom can.

How Come, Huh?

The illustrations to the right should help a lot. A water molecule is made up of three atoms, two hydrogens and one oxygen. The two hydrogen atoms sit on top of the oxygen atom and create a positive charge on that end of the molecule. This also exposes the oxygen atom, which has a negative charge. With positive charges on one end and negative on the other, you have a little magnet.

The cotton string absorbed the water when it was dunked in the can. As the water from the can started to trickle out on to the string the water molecules in the string were attracted to the water molecules sliding down the string. Another word for this attraction is cohesion.

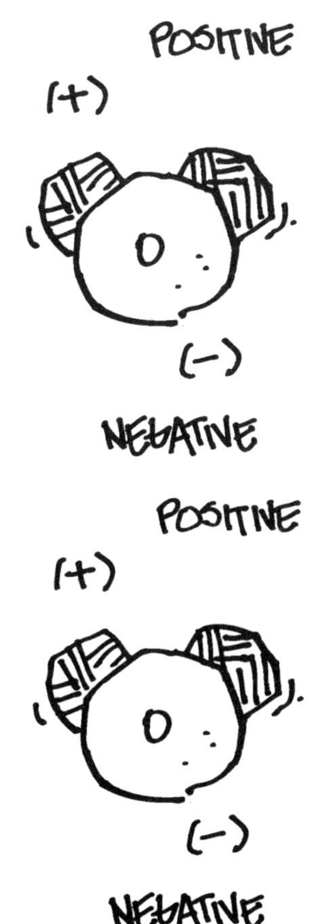

Science Fair Extensions

77. Try other kinds of transport media like fishing line, steel wire, guitar strings, fabric strips and compare your results.

Centering a Cork

The Experiment

It is a well-known fact that when a small cork is placed on the surface of the water in your Toobe, it always migrates to the side of the cylinder. Despite several stern conversations and much consternation, you can never seem to get it to stay put in the middle of the Toobe no matter what you do.

Your task is to figure out a way to get that cork to stay in the middle of the Toobe without having anything physically hold it in place other than water and air.

Materials

1 Toobe or other container
1 Small cork
1 Box of paper clips
1 Plastic, 1 mL pipette
Water

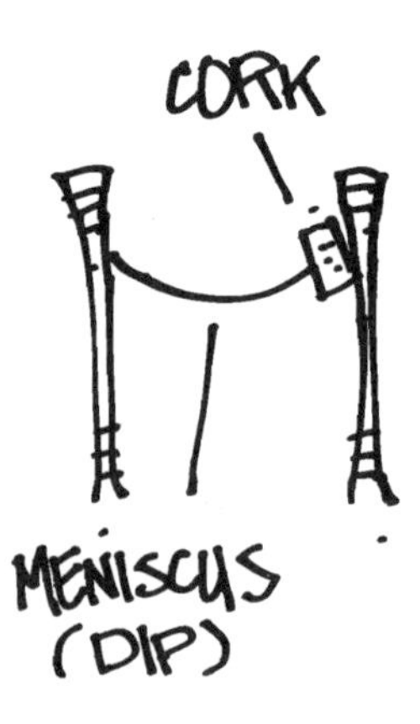

Procedure

1. Fill the Toobe almost completely full of water and gently place the cork in the center. The cork will migrate to the side of the Toobe because the water inside the Toobe forms a dip, called a meniscus. Since the cork is less dense than the water, it will always float to the highest point on the water. In this case it is the side of the Toobe.

2. Slowly add paper clips to the water until it starts to form a bulge and the water looks like it might spill out on to the table. When the bulge in the water starts to appear, you will notice that the cork begins to float to the highest point in the water, which now is the top of the bulge and also the center of the Toobe. Mission accomplished.

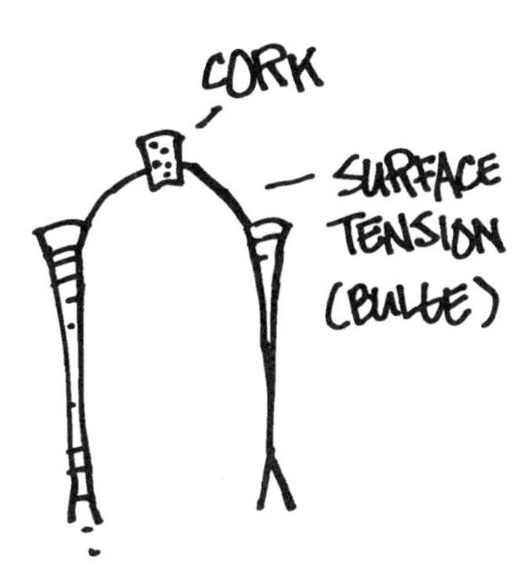

3. Empty the paper clips, refill the water, taking it almost all the way to the top once again, and replace the cork. Time for round two. Using the plastic pipette, slowly add water instead of paper clips to the Toobe. As you do this, you will notice that the cohesion of the water molecules starts to form that bulge again. As you keep adding the water, you will notice that the cork, which likes to float to the "highest" point in the water, will eventually be floating in the middle of the container directly on top of the bulge created by the surface tension in the water.

How Come, Huh?

The key to this is the fact that water molecules behave like little magnets. Because they are free to spin and rotate in any direction they can line themselves up, positive atttracted to negative, and form a skin or layer of magnetically attracted molecules, almost like a big net. As the water level inside the Toobe grows and starts to exceed the capacity of the Toobe, the water molecules can still hang on to one another because of this weak electromagnetic attraction. That is what forms the bulge in containers full of water.

Now, being less dense than the water, the cork will always float to the highest point in the water. When the water level is below the rim of the Toobe, the water forms a dip, called a meniscus, inside the container. With a meniscus, the highest point of the water in the container is along the perimeter of the cylinder so the cork always migrates to the side.

Centering a Cork

By adding paper clips or more water, either of which displaces the existing water beyond the capacity of the Toobe forming a dome and creating a high point in the water. The cork will always float to the highest point in the water, so it heads to the top of the dome that is also in the middle of the Toobe.

Science Fair Extensions

78. Predict if this experiment will work with a liquid that does not have surface tension and then perform the experiment to support your hypothesis.

79. Try the experiment with other objects that float and see if you get the same results. Now that we think of it maybe you could also try adding a drop of vegetable oil.

Obedient Bubbles

The Experiment

A rubber balloon will be rubbed on someone's head, preferably with shoulder-length, fine hair, but any pile of clean hair will work. The rubbing action collects free electrons from the surface of the hair. As these electrons pile up on the surface of the balloon, the hair sheaths will begin to float and repel one another.

You can stick this charged balloon to the ceiling, walls, passing dogs, or wool sweaters. However, the point of this lab is to explore the electrostatic effect of an accumulated charge on a soap bubble. A soap bubble simply being a drip of water that got stretched out into a sphere.

Materials

1 Rubber balloon, round, 9"
1 Person, full head of hair works best
1 Bottle of bubble solution

Procedure

Before we start, it is important to note that this experiment—like all electrostatic experiments—works best in low humidity.

1. Inflate the balloon and tie it off. If this is hard to do, have someone lend you a lung.

Obedient Bubbles

2. You can either perform this experiment on yourself or select a friend to volunteer and help you out. For best results use someone who has shoulder-length hair that is free of mousse, hair spray, or gel. Fine hair tends to work better than coarse hair.

And remember, blondes may have more fun, but not until you rub their heads with a rubber balloon.

3. Rub the balloon back and forth all over the hair. As you rub, occasionally lift the balloon up off their hair about 6 inches. Their hair will follow. After about 30 seconds of rubbing, the hair sheaths should be sticking up and floating all around the place.

4. Take the cap off the bubble solution and blow several bubbles up into the air. Hold the charged balloon just a couple of inches above the soap bubbles, and you will find that several of them will be attracted toward the balloon. As the bubbles rise toward the balloon, you have to be careful to keep the balloon moving away or the bubble will zip right into the balloon and explode on the surface.

Select one bubble and practice bringing the balloon close to it. Get so that you can tug the bubble all over the classroom with the balloon. As long as you keep a safe distance, you will have a very obedient bubble.

5. If you want to have some fun, charge the balloon and bring it close the to head of the person who you stole the electrons from. Their hair will be instantly attracted to the balloon.

How Come, Huh?

Opposite charges (negative and positive) attract, and like charges (negative and negative) or (positive and positive) repel. It's the same way with magnets. The balloon has a huge negative charge because it has stolen all the loose electrons from the hair sheaths, and the hair has a huge positive charge because all of its electrons have been stolen. Balloon negative, hair positive: They attract. When you take the balloon out of the picture, the hair still tends to stand up on end. This is because each of the hair strands has a positive charge. Like charges repel, and since they can't stand each other, they get as far away from one another as is possible. In this case they stand on end.

The bubble is attracted to the static charge on the balloon because our water molecule has one side that is positively charged and one side that is negatively charged. Opposites attract.

Science Fair Extensions

80. Experiment with the shape of the balloon and see if a particular kind of shape—round, cylinder, wiggly—makes a difference in how the charge is collected, stored, or shared.

81. Find other materials to make "balloons" out of. Try plastic grocery sacks, dry-cleaning bags, paper grocery bags, mylar balloons, or aluminum foil balloons. Rate them on their ability to collect and distribute a charge.

One-Way Cheesecloth

The Experiment

If you take a piece of cheesecloth and hold it up to the light, you will see thousands of little holes. Despite the fact that there are all of these holes, cheesecloth makes a very effective lid for a container of water. Weird but true.

This lab will allow you to explore surface tension—the ability of water molecules to hang on to one another, in small spaces. In this case you are going to explore the characteristics of cheesecloth and try to explain the fact that water can flow freely through cheesecloth in one direction but not in the other.

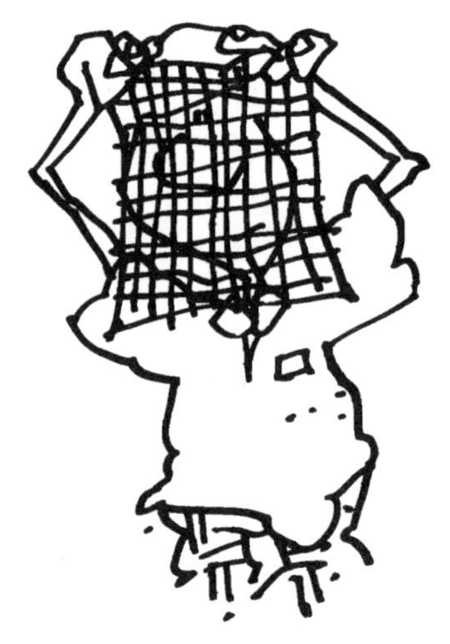

Materials

1 Toobe or other container
1 Cheesecloth, 6" by 6" square
1 Elastic
1 Drinking glass, 10 to 12 oz.
Water

Procedure

1. Starting with an empty Toobe, or other container, place the twice folded cheesecloth over the opening, pull it tight, and put an elastic over it to hold it in place.

2. Fill the drinking glass with water and pour it directly into the Toobe from a height of about 10 inches. You will notice that you have no trouble filling your Toobe with water.

3. Holding your Toobe over a sink or outside where you can make a mess, quickly flip it upside down with your hand on top of the cheesecloth. Slowly remove your hand and observe what happens to the water in the Toobe.

4. Flip the Toobe over again, and this time when you invert it, you will not need to use your hand to support the cheesecloth, provided that you flip the whole contraption quickly enough.

5. With the Toobe upside down examine the individual holes in the cheesecloth.

How Come, Huh?

When you are pouring the water into the Toobe, it has lots of energy. Starting out 10 inches above the Toobe gives it lots of potential energy. As the water is pulled by gravity toward the Toobe, it speeds up and has even more energy, so that when it hits the holes in the cheesecloth, it zips right on through and into the bottom of the container. That explains the first half of the experiment.

A couple of things happen in the second part of the experiment. First, as you flip the Toobe upside down, your hand temporarily blocks the water from falling by holding it inside the container. This gives the water time to clog the holes in the cheesecloth, which it does because of that natural attraction between water molecules—it's that magnet thing. So the water molecules are hanging on to each other, plugging the holes in the cheesecloth. But we still don't know why the water doesn't come gushing out of the Toobe when you remove your hand. This is because when you flip the Toobe upside down, you are actually creating a partial vacuum at the top of the Toobe.

One-Way Cheesecloth

So here's the scenario: Water is plugging the holes of the cheesecloth, which basically makes a single uniform surface. A couple of pounds of water and a little bit of air pressure inside the Toobe are pushing *down* on the cheesecloth; 14.7 pounds per square inch of air pressure are pushing *up* on the cheesecloth. The water does not have enough weight or energy to push the cheesecloth out of the way so that it can escape—hence a one-way cheesecloth.

Science Fair Extensions

82. Repeat this experiment using an index card, sheet of cardboard, piece of aluminum foil, or other surface of your choice in place of the cheesecloth and see if you can replicate the results.

83. Repeat this experiment using a dry piece of cheesecloth, but this time when you flip the whole concoction over, do not place your hand over the opening at first. Explain your results.

84. Try other kinds of materials—cotton, silk, rayon, burlap—and see if you can duplicate the results that you got with the cheesecloth. Compare the size of the holes in the fabric with the effectiveness of the fabric as a cloth and try to determine if that has anything at all to do with this experiment.

Paper Boat Race

The Experiment

Surface tension is the secret to this lab and also what this lab is all about. The design of a small boat is cut out from an index card. This boat is placed in a pie tin full of water and nothing happens. It is removed and a drop of soap is placed in the groove cut in the back of the boat, and when it is placed in the water a second time—Ka-zing!—off it goes.

Materials

1 Index card
Water
1 Pair of scissors
1 9" Pie tin
1 1 oz. Bottle of liquid soap

Procedure

1. Cut a triangle from the index card: 2 inches high and 1 inch wide should do it, but it doesn't really matter, you can experiment with other designs.

2. Cut a smaller triangle out of the bottom of the boat. Use the drawing to the right as a guide. This is where the motor goes.

3. Fill the pie tin with clean water. Place your boat in the water near the edge of the pie tin. It is not going to go anywhere. The problem, which is probably obvious, is that there's not any gas in the motor.

Paper Boat Race

3. Take your boat out of the water for servicing. Place a drop of the liquid detergent on you finger and touch it just inside the V notch of the boat. Put the boat back in the water, soapy side down, and it will jet across the water much to the delight and amazement of your friends.

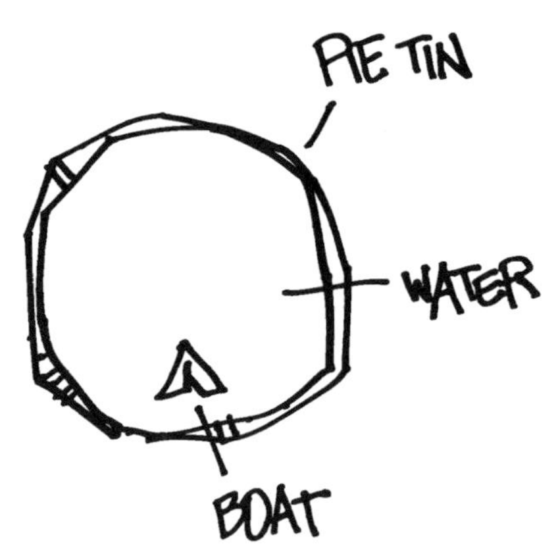

4. Make a second boat. Add a drop of soap to the motor before you place it in the same, previously used, pan of water. Put the boat in the water, soapy side down and observe what happens. Record your observations in the spaces below.

Data & Observations

Draw a picture of the paths that your boats took the first and second times that you placed them in the water.

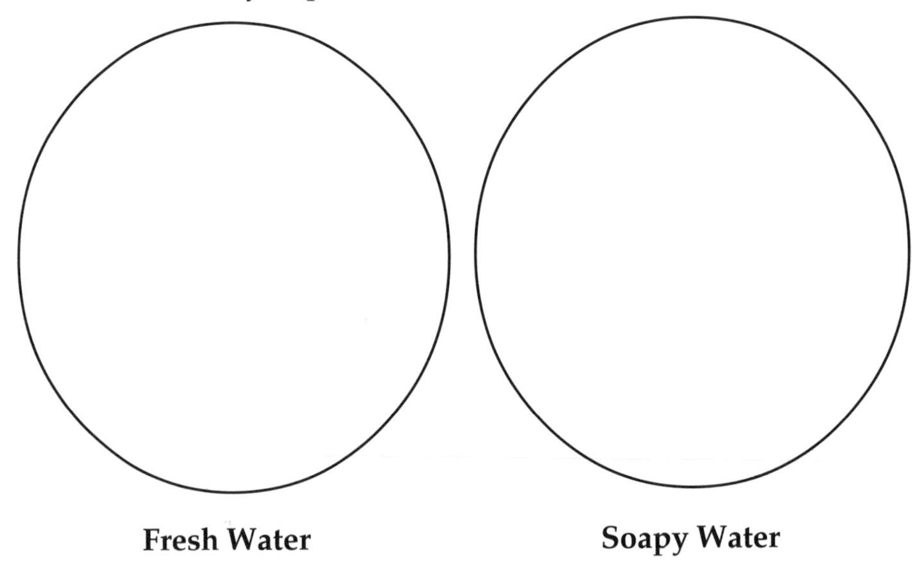

Fresh Water **Soapy Water**

How Come, Huh?

If we could see a water molecule, it would look like Mickey Mouse's head. Because the hydrogen atoms are stacked toward the top and are not linear, the molecule has a positive end (the ears) and a negative end (the head). Because of this characteristic, water is called a polar molecule, meaning that it acts like a little tiny magnet.

But for now, imagine that the entire surface of the water is made up of these little water-molecule magnets all lined up hanging on to each other. This is the current theory explaining surface tension.

The reason the boat zips across the water is the soap molecules like to split up the water molecules' attraction to one another. When they do this, the water molecules spin like crazy and bump into one another and anything else that may be there, like a piece of cardboard cut into the shape of a boat. All of this spinning and bumping pushes the boat forward.

However, surface tension is kind of like a rubber balloon. Once you pop the balloon that is all she wrote—once you burst the surface tension you cannot repeat the experiment.

Science Fair Extensions

85. You have an entire world of materials at your disposal. Explore this idea using different kinds of materials for your boat.

86. Design an experiment that proves or disproves the idea that temperature has an effect on the surface tension of the water in the pie tin.

Scared Pepper

The Experiment

A pie tin full of clean water is sprinkled with pepper so that it covers the entire surface. A drop of soap is added to the center of the pan, and the pepper shoots to the perimeter of the tin.

If you are reading the book in order, then you have just figured out that we are trying another experiment demonstrating the characteristics of surface tension. This particular idea supports and is even more effective in presenting the idea than the previous lab.

Materials

1 Pie tin, 9" to 12"
1 Pepper shaker with ground pepper
1 1 oz. Bottle of liquid soap
Water

Procedure

1. Fill the pie tin with clean water from the tap and sprinkle the pepper evenly over the surface. Use the illustration to the right as a guide.

2. Add a drop of liquid soap to the center of the pan and observe what happens to the pepper. Record your observations in the space provided on the next page.

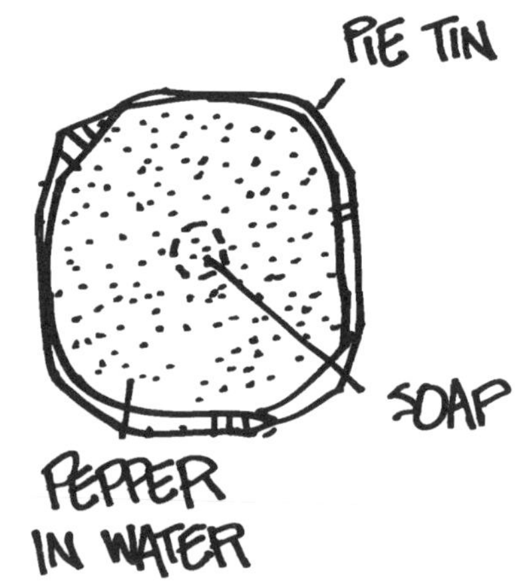

Data & Observations

Draw a picture of the experiment before and after you added the drop of liquid soap.

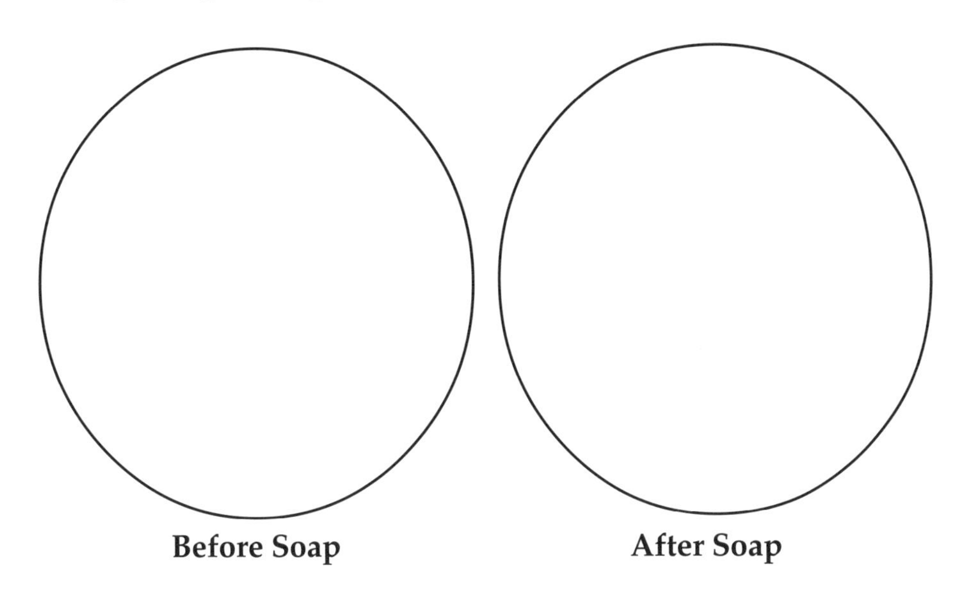

How Come, Huh?

If we could see a water molecule, it would look like Mickey Mouse's head. Because the hydrogen atoms are stacked toward the top and are not linear, the molecule has a positive end (the ears) and a negative end (the head). Because of this characteristic, water is called a polar molecule, meaning that it acts like a little tiny magnet.

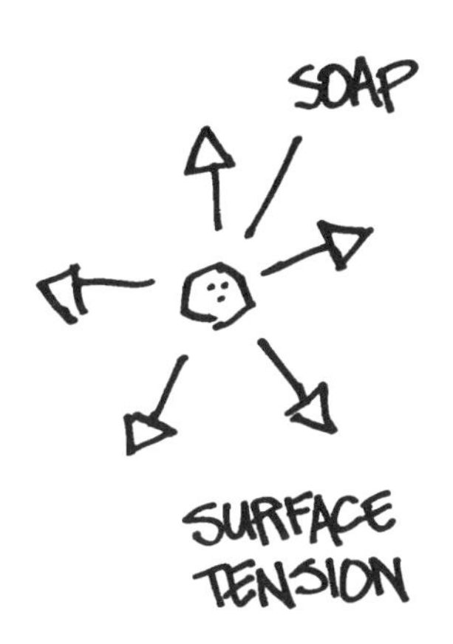

But for now, imagine that the entire surface of the water is made up of these little water-molecule magnets all lined up hanging on to each other. This is the current theory explaining surface tension.

Scared Pepper

The soap once again gets in between the water molecules and causes all kinds of confusion. The soap breaks through the skin of the water. Think of it like a pin popping a balloon. The pin goes in and the balloon collapses. The soap goes in and the "water skin" collapses, taking the pepper with it as it retreats to the edge of the tin.

Science Fair Extensions

87. There are all kinds of things that float on the surface of water: sawdust, chalk, pepper, and a huge variety of spices like paprika, dill, sage, and oregano for starters. Do any of these items have an effect on the way this experiment plays out. Make a list of 10 items, try them, and see if there is any change.

88. Design an experiment that proves or disproves the idea that the shape of the container has an effect on the surface tension of the water in the container. Try square baking dishes, round bowls, oblong vegetable dishes, funky sand toys like fish, octopi, and castles.

89. Explore to see if there are additives that you can add to the water that make this experiment work better. Oil? Salt? Food coloring? Make a list of things that you would like to try and see if any of them change the end result.

Exploding Oil Drops

The Experiment

Again, surface tension appears before us to present yet another spin on this idea of electrostatic attraction between molecules.

Your task in this lab is to figure out a way to get a drop of vegetable oil from the center of the Toobe, where it is most comfortable, to the edges—where it is less likely to reside on any given day.

Materials

1 Toobe or other container
1 1 oz. Bottle of vegetable oil
1 1 oz. Bottle of liquid soap
1 Pipette, 1 mL
1 Packet of pepper
Water

Procedure

1. Fill your Toobe, or other container almost full of water, leave an inch or so near the top.

2. Using a pipette, add a large drop of vegetable oil to the surface of the water. The size of a dime is good. Gently tip the Toobe back and forth, then side to side, and you will see that no matter what you do, the oil drop always moves back to the center. Draw a picture of what you see in the Toobe.

Exploding Oil Drops

3. Now, add a small drop of liquid soap to the center of the oil drop. There should be a dramatic change in the shape and the position of the oil drop. Draw a picture of what you see in the space provided below.

Data & Observations

Draw a picture of the experiment before and after you added the drop of liquid soap.

Before Soap **After Soap**

How Come, Huh?

The oil floats on the surface of the water in the Toobe because it is less dense than the water molecules. When you tipped the Toobe back and forth, the oil was just like a boat riding a wave in the ocean.

The soap was a different story altogether. Soap molecules have one end that loves to be in the water, this is called the hydrophilic or water-loving end; and it has another end that is scared to death of water and hates to be in it, called the hydrophobic or water-fearing end.

When a molecule of soap is added to the water, the water-loving end dives into the water, splitting the oil drop into lots of pieces and at the same time interrupting the surface tension. It is a lot like puncturing a balloon with a pin. The balloon starts to separate at the pin hole and moves away from the point of entry. This is why the oil drop appears to burst

Science Fair Extensions

90. This experiment can be demonstrated using any small object, as well as several other liquids that float on water. Start with the list we have provided and see if you can find a total of 10 things that will demonstrate this idea.

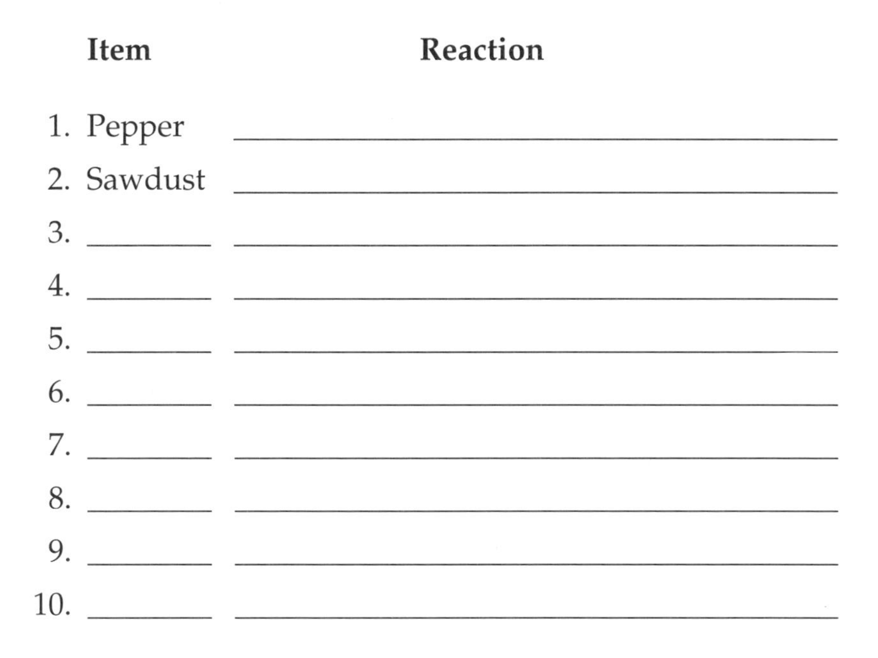

Item	Reaction
1. Pepper	________________
2. Sawdust	________________
3. ________	________________
4. ________	________________
5. ________	________________
6. ________	________________
7. ________	________________
8. ________	________________
9. ________	________________
10. ________	________________

Jumping Paper

The Experiment

Paper does not normally jump. In fact, in this experiment, despite the name that we have given the lab, the paper still does not jump. However, we are going to take advantage of the attraction between water molecules to create the appearance of jumping.

A piece of paper is going to be folded into an accordion shape. The bottom fold of the accordion will be soaked in water and then removed. The wet end of the paper will then be slowly lowered toward a pan full of water with very surprising and pleasing results—but no jumping.

Materials

1 Strip of paper, 1" by 8"
1 Pie tin
Water

Procedure

1. If you are using an entire sheet of paper, cut a strip of paper from the edge of the sheet using a pair of scissors. It should be about 1 inch wide and 8 inches long.

2. Using the illustration to the right, fold the paper into an accordion shape. The folds should be about 1 inch apart. The bottom fold should be pointing straight down.

3. Fill the pie tin with water. Lower the piece of paper toward the water, but do not let it touch the surface. Look for a reaction. If you do see something, try again, because the paper should stay perfectly still with the exception of the occasional wiggle that is caused by your hand moving.

4. Lower the last fold to the water and get it wet. Lift the accordion out of the water and then lower it to the surface again, but do not put it in the water. As you get closer and closer, you will notice that the paper eventually "jumps" into the water that is in the pie tin.

How Come, Huh?

It is important to know what a water molecule looks like and how it behaves to understand what is going on here. Water molecules are naturally attracted to each other. As you can see, they have a positive end and a negative end just like a magnet. The little atoms on the top that look like Mickey Mouse ears have a positive charge, or act like the north end of a magnet, and the big atoms at the bottom have a negative charge and act like the south end of a magnet.

Because they have this shape, the water molecules all line up and hang on to each other magnetically when they get close to one another. When the end of the paper is dipped into the water, the water molecules all line up inside the paper. As the paper is lowered to the surface of the water, the water starts to feel the pull of the water molecules in the paper.

When the paper gets close enough, the water molecules in the pie tin tug on the water molecules in the paper magnetically and pull them down into the water to be with their other water-molecule buddies.

Jumping Paper

Science Fair Extensions

Hopefully, you were surprised and pleased with the reaction between the wet paper and the water. This particular lab is quite often used to demonstrate how to generate a new and original hypothesis. Here are some examples of the ways that you can tweak this lab:

91. Change the liquid level that was in the pie tin. See if the level of the water has anything at all to do with the outcome.

92. Change the liquid to something new. Try oil, salt water, soda pop, rubbing alcohol, coffee, tea, and other liquids.

93. Change the temperature of the liquid up or down, and see if that affects the experiment in a positive or negative way

94. Add something to the water. Salt is a good starting point; sugar is also fun, but there are tons of chemicals that can be added to water to create useful solutions. You can also run an electric current through the water.

95. Change the material (paper) that was folded and dipped to try something new. Use aluminum foil, plastic wrap, construction paper, cardboard, fabric, wood, or a host of other things.

96. Change the shape of the paper and see if a skinnier sheet, a fatter sheet, a longer sheet, or a curlicue sheet has any affect on the outcome of the experiment.

Giant Bubble Machine

The Experiment

There it is, staring at you. A puddle of soapy solution on the kitchen table—mocking your bubble-making abilities. You are to take an ordinary straw and produce a bubble over a foot in diameter.

If a soapy solution is poured on a smooth surface—like a kitchen counter top—and a straw is placed directly over the puddle, huge bubbles can be created by gently blowing into the straw. Once you have mastered the art of making giant bubbles, you can then proceed to bubble trains, bubble apartments, bubble domes, and other assorted configurations.

Materials

1	2-Liter pop bottle
10	Cups of water
1	Cup Joy™ or Dawn™*
1	1 oz. Bottle of glycerin
1	Tablespoon
1	Straw
1	Hard, smooth surface

*According to full-time bubbleologists, these two brands of soap work the best when it comes to making long-lasting bubbles. The glycerin can be purchased at your local drugstore, but it has been rumored that corn syrup works well, also. The longer you save your solution, the better it tends to get, kind of like fine wine. Have fun.

Procedure

1. The first thing that you are going to want to do is mix up your bubble solution. Start with a clean, empty, 2-liter pop bottle. Fill the bottle with 5 cups of warm water. Add 1 cup of liquid soap, your choice. Add 1 tablespoon of glycerin, cap the mixture, and shake. Remove the cap and add 5 more cups of warm water, cap and shake a second time, and you are ready to go.

2. Pour a small puddle of soap solution, about the size of a large pancake, out on to the countertop in your kitchen or bathroom. Hold the straw almost upright and place it in the middle of the puddle. Begin to gently blow through the straw, and you will see a dome begin to form.

3. Try making bubbles inside of bubbles. Blow a large bubble and then gently remove the straw and dip it into the solution on the table and reinsert it into the bubble. Begin blowing again and another bubble will appear. It is also possible to make bubble colonies, chains of bubbles, and two-story bubbles, but rather than tell you how, I'll let you experiment and discover this on your own.

4. When you are all done, wipe the mess up with a washcloth and toss the straw in the garbage.

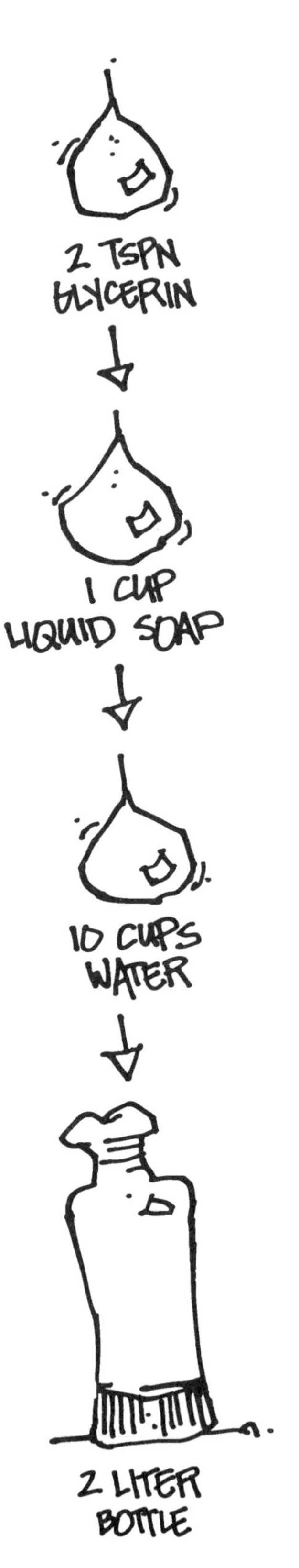

Giant Bubble Machine

Data & Observations

Draw pictures of the bubble creations that you created. Draw them from the perspective of looking down on top of the surface where the bubbles are being created.

How Come, Huh?

When you placed the straw on the table, you were actually submersing it in a shallow pool of soap solution. As you blew into the straw, the air that was forced down into the other end was actually trapped by the water and soap. As long as you did not blow too quickly or make a unexpected motions, you were able to create giant bubbles, bubbles inside bubbles, and bubble colonies. The reason for this is simple:

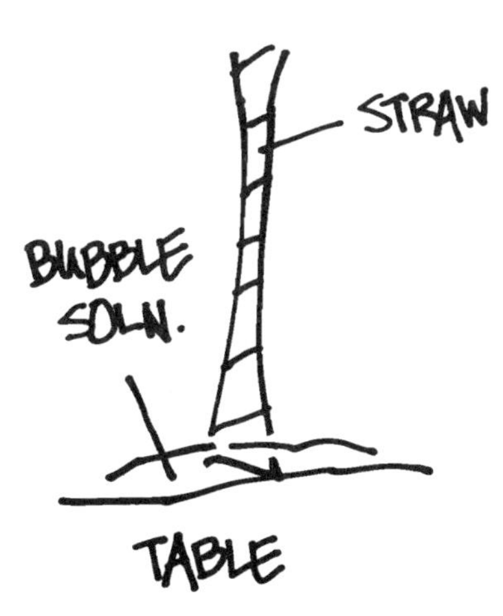

Giant Bubble Machine

A soap bubble is simply a drip of water that has been stretched out into a sphere. The only way to do this is to loosen that magnetic attraction that we talked about in the first part of this section. The best way to do this is to add soap.

Soap is an interesting molecule. It is actually a long chain of carbon and hydrogen atoms. At one end is a clump of atoms that like to be in the water (hydrophilic, or water-loving), and at the other end is another clump of molecules that can't stand to be in the water (hydrophobic, or afraid of water). When soap is dropped into the water, the end of the molecule that likes to be in the water wiggles in between the water molecules, causing them to bump and move around, and the end that hates the water sticks up out of the water. This loosens the water molecules up so that you can blow bubbles. Glycerin (a kind of sugar water) is added to give the walls of the bubble strength.

As the air is forced on to the table top, the bubbles begin to develop. They will increase in size until they pop due to evaporation, which thins the sides of the bubble until it can no longer support its own weight.

Science Fair Extensions

97. Alter the shape of the end of the straw and see if that affects the bubbles that you produce on the surface.

98. Try creating bubbles on a curved surface, like the inside of a very large bowl, a sink, or snow disk. See how that shape affects the sizes and shapes of the bubbles you blow.

The Instant Bubbler

The Experiment

A skinny straw is inserted into a solution of soap and water. When you exhale, gas bubbles become trapped at the surface of the water, forming a foam made out of very large bubbles. Another colloid has been created, and this is another mechanical foam as well. Just think, you did this as a kid with your milk and now it's actually a science experiment. This getting older stuff isn't bad at all.

Next, after you clean your cup out, you are going to add a small piece of dry ice to the Toobe. The dry ice is going to produce bubbles of carbon dioxide gas that you can see rising, very rapidly, through the surface of the water and bursting. When you add a squirt of soap to the water, the carbon dioxide will get trapped in the soapy water, forming a foggy foam that grows and oozes out of the cup and down the sides until it pops.

Materials

1 Straw
1 1 oz. Bottle of liquid soap
1 5" Pie tin
1 Toobe or other container
1 Small piece of dry ice (Adult supervision needed)
1 Pair of gloves
Water

Procedure

1. For the first part of the experiment, fill the Toobe, or other container, half full with water. Add three squirts of liquid soap. Mix them into solution with the straw.

The Instant Bubbler

2. Insert the straw down into the Toobe and start to blow bubbles in the solution. You will immediately notice that a herd of bubbles will start to rise up out of the container toward you. Blow until you are thoroughly entertained and then clean the Toobe and your area when you are done making observations.

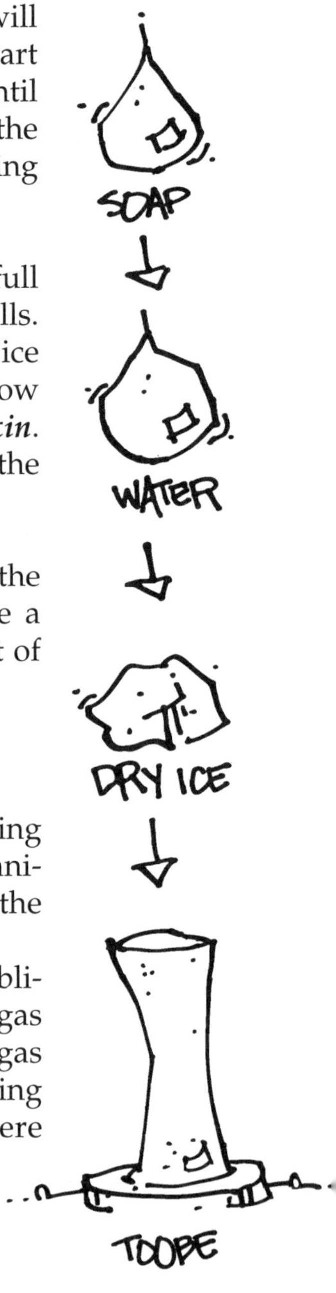

3. This time fill the Toobe three-fourths full with water and put it in the pie tin to catch any spills. Ask your teacher or a parent to add a piece of dry ice to the water. ***Dry ice*** is very cold, 112 degrees below zero, and ***should never be touched with bare skin***. Observe the bubbles of gas that are produced by the chunk of dry ice.

4. Add a couple of squirts of liquid soap to the water in the container and you will now have a major production of bubbles oozing up and out of the container.

How Come, Huh?

The first time around you were producing bubbles by blowing into a straw. A kind of mechanical foam: The air would leave your lungs, enter the liquid and then be pushed to the surface.

In the second instance, the dry ice was sublimating—changing directly from a solid to a gas without taking time to become a liquid. The gas formed bubbles at the bottom of the tube and being lighter than the surrounding liquid they were pushed to the top of the Toobe.

Once the dry ice hit the top of the Toobe, the extremely cold carbon dioxide came in contact with the water-rich, room-temperature air and caused the water to immediately condense or form a mini-cloud. This cloud was trapped in the liquid by the soap bubbles and slid down the side of the container.

Science Fair Extensions

99. Try this experiment without the soap and see how it affects the outcome. Explain why the soap is important.

100. Explain how this contraption is difference from the soap bubble machines that are used on dance floors and behind big bands. Figure out a way to combine the two processes to make an even more efficient bubble machine.

101. Experiment with the recipe for the soap solution as well as the size of the straw, the opening on the straw, and other factors to create the longest, largest, string of bubbles.

Science Fair Projects

•

A Step-by-Step Guide: From Idea to Presentation

Science Fair Projects

Ah, the impending science fair project—a good science fair project has the following five characteristics:

1. The student must come up with an *original* question.
2. That *original* question must be suited to an experiment in order to provide an answer.
3. The *original* idea is outlined with just one variable isolated.
4. The *original* experiment is performed and documented using the scientific method.
5. A presentation of the *original* idea in the form of a lab write-up and display board is completed.

Science Fair Projects

As simple as science fair versus science project sounds, it gets screwed up millions of times a year by sweet, unsuspecting students who are counseled by sweet, unknowing, and probably just as confused parents.

To give you a sense of contrast we have provided a list of legitimate science fair projects and then reports that do not qualify. We will also add some comments in italics that should help clarify why they do or do not qualify in the science fair project department.

Science Fair Projects

1. Temperature and the amount of time it takes mealworms to change to beetles.

Great start. We have chosen a single variable that is easy to measure: temperature. From this point forward the student can read, explore, and formulate an original question that is the foundation for the project.

A colleague of mine actually did a similar type of experiment for his master's degree. His topic: The rate of development of fly larva in cow poop as a function of temperature. No kidding. He found out that the warmer the temperature of the poop the faster the larva developed into flies.

2. The effect of different concentrations of soapy water on seed germination.

Again, wonderful. Measuring the concentration of soapy water. This leads naturally into original questions and a good project.

3. Crystal size and the amount of sugar in the solution.

This could lead into other factors such as exploring the temperature of the solution, the size of the solution container, and other variables that may affect crystal growth. Opens a lot of doors.

vs. Science Reports

4. Helicopter rotor size and the speed at which it falls.

Size also means surface area, which is very easy to measure. The student who did this not only found the mathematical threshold with relationship to air friction, but she had a ton of fun.

5. The ideal ratio of baking soda to vinegar to make a fire extinguisher.

Another great start. Easy to measure and track, leads to a logical question that can either be supported or refuted with the data.

Each of those topics *measures* one thing such as the amount of sugar, the concentration of soapy water, or the ideal size. If you start with an idea that allows you to measure something, then you can change it, ask questions, explore, and ultimately make a *prediction*, also called a *hypothesis*, and experiment to find out if you are correct. Here are some well-meaning but misguided entries:

Science Reports, not Projects

1. Dinosaurs!

OK, great. Everyone loves dinosaurs but where is the experiment? Did you find a new dinosaur? Is Jurassic Park alive and well, and we are headed there to breed, drug, or in some way test them? Probably not. This was a report on T. rex. Cool, but not a science fair project. And judging by the protest that this kid's mom put up when the kid didn't get his usual "A", it is a safe bet that she put a lot of time in and shared in the disappointment.

More Reports &

2. Our Friend the Sun

Another very large topic, no pun intended. This could be a great topic. Sunlight is fascinating. It can be split, polarized, reflected, refracted, measured, collected, converted. However, this poor kid simply chose to write about the size of the sun, regurgitate facts about its features, cycles, and other astrofacts while simultaneously offending the American Melanoma Survivors Society. Just kidding about that last part.

3. Smokers' Poll

A lot of folks think that they are headed in the right direction here. Again, it depends on how the kid attacks the idea. Are they going to single out race? Heredity? Shoe size? What exactly are they after here? The young lady who did this report chose to make it more of a psychology-studies effort than a scientific report. She wanted to know family income, if they fought with their parents, how much stress was on the job, and so on. All legitimate concerns but not placed in the right slot.

4. The Majestic Moose

If you went out and caught the moose, drugged it to see the side effects for disease control, or even mated it with an elk to determine if you could create an animal that would become the spokesanimal for the Alabama Dairy Farmers' Got Melk? promotion, that would be fine. But, another fact-filled report should be filed with the English teacher.

5. How Tadpoles Change into Frogs

Great start, but they forgot to finish the statement. We know how tadpoles change into frogs. What we don't know is how tadpoles change into frogs if they are in an altered environment, if they are hatched out of cycle, if they are stuck under the tire of an off-road vehicle blatantly driving through a protected wetland area. That's what we want to know. How tadpoles change into frogs, if, when, or under what measurable circumstances.

Now that we have beat the chicken squat out of this introduction, we are going to show you how to pick a topic that can be adapted to become a successful science fair project after one more thought.

One Final Comment

A Gentle Reminder

Quite often I discuss the scientific method with moms and dads, teachers and kids, and get the impression that, according to their understanding, there is one, and only one, scientific method. This is not necessarily true. There are lots of ways to investigate the world we live in and on.

Paleontologists dig up dead animals and plants but have no way to conduct experiments on them. They're dead. Albert Einstein, the most famous scientist of the last century and probably on everybody's starting five of all time, never did experiments. He was a theoretical physicist, which means that he came up with a hypothesis, skipped over collecting materials for things like black holes and space-time continuums, didn't experiment on anything or even collect data. He just went straight from hypothesis to conclusion, and he's still considered part of the scientific community. You'll probably follow the six steps we outline but keep an open mind.

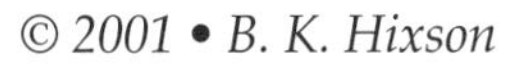

Project Planner

This outline is designed to give you a specific set of time lines to follow as you develop your science fair project. Most teachers will give you 8 to 11 weeks notice for this kind of assignment. We are going to operate from the shorter time line with our suggested schedule, which means that the first thing you need to do is get a calendar.

A. The suggested time to be devoted to each item is listed in parentheses next to that item. Enter the date of the Science Fair and then, using the calendar, work backward entering dates.

B. As you complete each item, enter the date that you completed it in the column between the goal (due date) and project item.

Goal	*Completed*	*Project Item*
		1. *Generate a Hypothesis* (2 weeks)
________	________	Review Idea Section, pp. 195–197
________	________	Try Several Experiments
________	________	Hypothesis Generated
________	________	Finished Hypothesis Submitted
________	________	Hypothesis Approved
		2. Gather Background Information (1 week)
________	________	Concepts/Discoveries Written Up
________	________	Vocabulary/Glossary Completed
________	________	Famous Scientists in Field

& Time Line

Goal	*Completed*	*Project Item*
		3. Design an Experiment (1 week)
________	________	Procedure Written
________	________	Lab Safety Review Completed
________	________	Procedure Approved
________	________	Data Tables Prepared
________	________	Materials List Completed
________	________	Materials Acquired
		4. Perform the Experiment (2 weeks)
________	________	Scheduled Lab Time
		5. Collect and Record Experimental Data (part of 4)
________	________	Data Tables Completed
________	________	Graphs Completed
________	________	Other Data Collected and Prepared
		6. Present Your Findings (2 weeks)
________	________	Rough Draft of Paper Completed
________	________	Proofreading Completed
________	________	Final Report Completed
________	________	Display Completed
________	________	Oral Report Outlined on Index Cards
________	________	Practice Presentation of Oral Report
________	________	Oral Report Presentation
________	________	Science Fair Setup
________	________	Show Time!

Scientific Method
• Step 1 •
The Hypothesis

The Hypothesis

A hypothesis is an educated guess. It is a statement of what you think will probably happen. It is also the most important part of your science fair project because it directs the entire process. It determines what you study, the materials you will need, and how the experiment will be designed, carried out, and evaluated. Needless to say, you need to put some thought into this part.

There are four steps to generating a hypothesis:

Step One • Pick a Topic

Preferably something that you are interested in studying. We would like to politely recommend that you take a peek at physical science ideas (physics and chemistry) if you are a rookie and this is one of your first shots at a science fair project. These kinds of lab ideas allow you to repeat experiments quickly. There is a lot of data that can be collected, and there is a huge variety to choose from.

If you are having trouble finding an idea, all you have to do is pick up a compilation of science activities (like this one) and start thumbing through it. Go to the local library or head to a bookstore and you will find a wide and ever-changing selection to choose from. Find a topic that interests you and start reading. At some point an idea will catch your eye, and you will be off to the races.

Pick an Idea You Like

We hope you find an idea you like between the covers of this book. But we also realize that 1) there are more ideas than we have included in this book, and 2) other kinds of presentations, or methods of writing labs, may be just what you need to trigger a new idea or put a different spin on things. So, without further adieu, we introduce you to several additional titles that may be of help to you in developing a science fair project.

1. Simple Chemistry Experiments with Everyday Materials. Written by Louis V. Loesching. ISBN 0-8069-0688-x Published by Sterling. 128 pages.

One hundred and ten experiments all using common household items. This book covers crystals, solutions, matter, and a host of other topics including some fun puzzles at the end where you become a science detective and solve some mysteries. Great book for extending the ideas from *Junior Chemhead.*

2. Chemistry for Every Kid. Written by Janice Van Cleave. ISBN 0-471-62085-8 Published by John Wiley & Sons. 232 pages.

Part of her very popular "Science for Every Kid" series. This book has 101 hands-on science activities that cover a very broad range of experiments, some of which could double as electricity, fluid dynamics, thermodynamics, or mechanics experiments. Chapter topics include: matter, pH, gases, phase changes, solutions, heat, and acids and bases.

The experiments are all very simple, generally use easy-to-find household materials, and come with entertaining illustrations. Weak in the extension department, but you should have a handle on that after reading this book anyway.

3. Cool Chemistry. Great Experiments with Simple Stuff. Written by Steve W. Moje. ISBN 0-8069-6349-2. Published by Sterling. 96 pages.

This book has 56 cool chemistry experiments. The instructions are very clear and the illustrations help the reader get through the main ideas easily. Topics include physical properties of matter, mixtures and solutions, acids and bases, and food chemistry. It's a great place to pick up where *Chemhead* left off. Plenty of new ideas.

4. Chemistry Basics by Penny Raife Durant. ISBN 0-531-10971-2 Published by Franklin Watts. 32 pages.

If you have a younger student who really enjoyed the very basic ideas in this book, then Penny's book is for you. It has 12 simple experiments that reinforce ideas covered in *Chemhead*. You will explore adsorption and repulsion of water, density, solubility, the changes of state, and experiment with a little bit of chromatography. It has the best illustrations of the six reviewed on these pages.

5. Experiments with Bubbles by Robert Gardner ISBN 0-89490-666-6 Published by Enslow. 104 pages.

If you got a big kick out of the last section of this book and really want to delve into the science of bubbleology, then this is a great book. Gardner takes you through 36 different bubble-related experiments ranging from the chemistry of bubbles, geometry, design, properties of light, and tensile strength. You will be a bubblexpert when you are done with this book.

6. Science Projects about Kitchen Chemistry by Robert Gardner ISBN 0-89490-953-3 Published by Enslow. 128 pages.

Robert Gardner is a very well known science-educator who has written a wheelbarrow full of hands-on science books. This particular work contains 45 experiments that investigate the three major food groups, liquids, acids and bases, and a host of other ideas.

Develop an Original Idea

Step Two • Do the Lab

Choose a lab activity that looks interesting and try the experiment. Some kids make the mistake of thinking that all you have to do is find a lab in a book, repeat the lab, and you are on the gravy train with biscuit wheels. Your goal is to ask an ORIGINAL question, not repeat an experiment that has been done a bazillion times before.

As you do the lab, be thinking not only about the data you are collecting, but of ways you could adapt or change the experiment to find out new information. The point of the science fair project is to have you become an actual scientist and contribute a little bit of new knowledge to the world.

You know that they don't pay all of those engineers good money to sit around and repeat other people's lab work. The company wants new ideas so if you are able to generate and explore new ideas you become very valuable, not only to that company but to society. It is the question-askers that find cures for diseases, create new materials, figure out ways to make existing machines energy efficient, and change the way that we live. For the purpose of illustration, we are going to take a lab titled, "Prisms, Water Prisms." from another book, *Photon U*, and run it through the rest of the process. The lab uses a tub of water, an ordinary mirror, and light to create a prism that splits the light into the spectrum of a rainbow. Cool. Easy to do. Not expensive and open to all kinds of adaptations, including the four that we discuss on the next page.

Step Three • Bend, Fold, Spindle, & Mutilate Your Lab

Once you have picked out an experiment, ask if it is possible to do any of the following things to modify it into an original experiment. You want to try and change the experiment to make it more interesting and find out one new, small piece of information.

Heat it	Freeze it	Reverse it	Double it
Bend it	Invert it	Poison it	Dehydrate it
Drown it	Stretch it	Fold it	Ignite it
Split it	Irradiate it	Oxidize it	Reduce it
Chill it	Speed it up	Color it	Grease it
Expand it	Substitute it	Remove it	Slow it down

If you take a look at our examples, that's exactly what we did to the main idea. We took the list of 24 different things that you could do to an experiment—not nearly all of them by the way—and tried a couple of them out on the prism setup.

Double it: Get a second prism and see if you can continue to separate the colors farther by lining up a second prism in the rainbow of the first.

Reduce it: Figure out a way to gather up the colors that have been produced and mix them back together to produce white light again.

Reverse it: Experiment with moving the flashlight and paper closer to the mirror and farther away. Draw a picture and be able to predict what happens to the size and clarity of the rainbow image.

Substitute it: You can also create a rainbow on a sunny day using a garden hose with a fine-spray nozzle attached. Set the nozzle adjustment so that a fine mist is produced and move the mist around in the sunshine until you see the rainbow. This works better if the sun is lower in the sky; late afternoon is best.

Hypothesis Work Sheet

Step Three (Expanded) • Bend, Fold, Spindle Work Sheet

This work sheet will give you an opportunity to work through the process of creating an original idea.

A. Write down the lab idea that you want to mangle.

____

____

____

____

B. List the possible variables you could change in the lab.

i. ______________________

ii. ______________________

iii. ______________________

iv. ______________________

v. ______________________

C. Take one variable listed in section B and apply one of the 24 changes listed below to it. Write that change down and state your new lab idea in the space below. Do that with three more changes.

Heat it	Freeze it	Reverse it	Double it
Bend it	Invert it	Poison it	Dehydrate it
Drown it	Stretch it	Fold it	Ignite it
Split it	Irradiate it	Oxidize it	Reduce it
Chill it	Speed it up	Color it	Grease it
Expand it	Substitute it	Remove it	Slow it down

i. ______________________________________

____

____

____

ii. ____

____

____

____

iii. ____

____

____

____

iv. ____

____

____

____

Step Four • Create an Original Idea— Your Hypothesis

Your hypothesis should be stated as an opinion. You've done the basic experiment, you've made observations, you're not stupid. Put two and two together and make a PREDICTION. Be sure that you are experimenting with just a single variable.

A. State your hypothesis in the space below. List the variable.

i. ____

____

____

____

ii. Variable tested: ______________________

Sample Hypothesis Work Sheet

On the previous two pages is a work sheet that will help you develop your thoughts and a hypothesis. Here is sample of the finished product to help you understand how to use it.

A. Write down the lab idea that you want to mutilate.
A mirror is placed in a tub of water. A beam of light is focused through the water onto the mirror, producing a rainbow on the wall.

B. List the possible variables you could change in the lab.

i. **Source of light**
ii. **The liquid in the tub**
iii. **The distance from flashlight to mirror**

C. Take one variable listed in section B and apply one of the 24 changes to it. Write that change down and state your new lab idea in the space below.

The shape of the beam of light can be controlled by making and placing cardboard filters over the end of the flashlight. Various shapes such as circles, squares, and slits will produce different quality rainbows.

D. State your hypothesis in the space below. List the variable. Be sure that when you write the hypothesis you are stating an idea and not asking a question.

Hypothesis: The narrower the beam of light the tighter, brighter, and more focused the reflected rainbow will appear.

Variable tested: **The opening on the filter**

Scientific Method • Step 2 • Gather Information

Gather Information

Read about your topic and find out what we already know. Check books, videos, the Internet, and movies, talk with experts in the field, and molest an encyclopedia or two. Gather as much information as you can before you begin planning your experiment.

In particular, there are several things that you will want to pay special attention to and that should accompany any good science fair project.

A. Major Scientific Concepts

Be sure that you research and explain the main idea(s) that is /are driving your experiment. It may be a law of physics or chemical rule or an explanation of an aspect of plant physiology.

B. Scientific Words

As you use scientific terms in your paper, you should also define them in the margins of the paper or in a glossary at the end of the report. You cannot assume that everyone knows about geothermal energy transmutation in sulfur-loving bacterium. Be prepared to define some new terms for them... and scrub your hands really well when you are done if that is your project.

C. Historical Perspective

When did we first learn about this idea, and who is responsible for getting us this far? You need to give a historical perspective with names, dates, countries, awards, and other recognition.

Building a Research Foundation

1. This sheet is designed to help you organize your thoughts and give you some ideas on where to look for information on your topic. When you prepare your lab report, you will want to include the background information outlined below.

A. Major Scientific Concepts (Two is plenty.)

i. ____

____

____

____

ii. ____

____

____

____

B. Scientific Words (No more than 10)

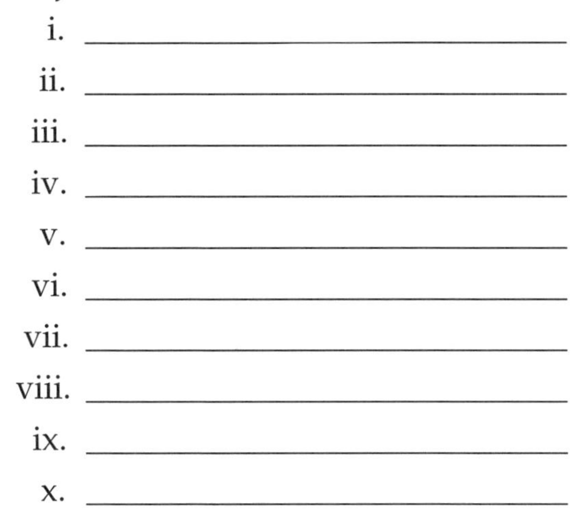

i. ______________________

ii. ______________________

iii. ______________________

iv. ______________________

v. ______________________

vi. ______________________

vii. ______________________

viii. ______________________

ix. ______________________

x. ______________________

C. Historical Perspective

Add this as you find it.

2. There are several sources of information that are available to help you fill in the details from the previous page.

A. Contemporary Print Resources
(Magazines, Newspapers, Journals)

i. ______________________________
ii. ______________________________
iii. ______________________________
iv. ______________________________
v. ______________________________
vi. ______________________________

B. Other Print Resources
(Books, Encyclopedias, Dictionaries, Textbooks)

i. ______________________________
ii. ______________________________
iii. ______________________________
iv. ______________________________
v. ______________________________
vi. ______________________________

C. Celluloid Resources
(Films, Filmstrips, Videos)

i. ______________________________
ii. ______________________________
iii. ______________________________
iv. ______________________________
v. ______________________________
vi. ______________________________

D. Electronic Resources:

(Internet Website Addresses, DVDs, MP3s)

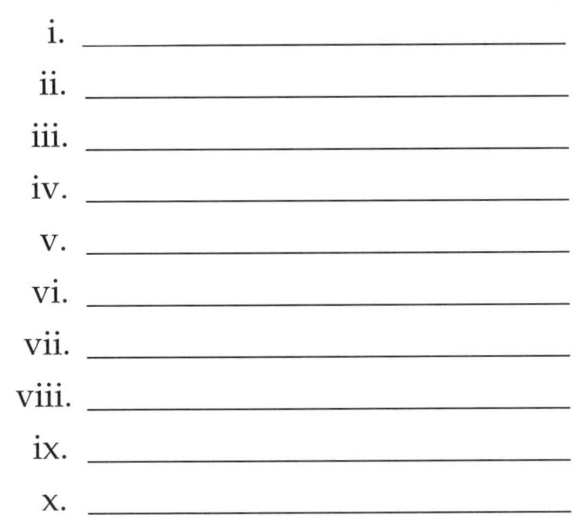

i. ______________________

ii. ______________________

iii. ______________________

iv. ______________________

v. ______________________

vi. ______________________

vii. ______________________

viii. ______________________

ix. ______________________

x. ______________________

E. Human Resources

(Scientists, Engineers, Professionals, Professors, Teachers)

i. ______________________

ii. ______________________

iii. ______________________

iv. ______________________

v. ______________________

vi. ______________________

You may want to keep a record of all of your research and add it to the back of the report as an Appendix. Some teachers who are into volume think this is really cool. Others, like myself, find it a pain in the tuchus. No matter what you do, be sure to keep an accurate record of where you find data. If you quote from a report word for word, be sure to give proper credit with either a footnote or parenthetical reference, this is very important for credibility and accuracy. This is will keep you out of trouble with plagiarism (copying without giving credit).

Scientific Method
• Step 3 •
Design Your Experiment

Acquire Your Lab Materials

The purpose of this section is to help you plan your experiment. You'll make a map of where you are going, how you want to get there, and what you will take along.

List the materials you will need to complete your experiment in the table below. Be sure to list multiples if you will need more than one item. Many science materials double as household items in their spare time. Check around the house before you buy anything from a science supply company or hardware store. For your convenience, we have listed some suppliers on page 19 of this book.

Material	Qty.	Source	$
1.			
2.			
3.			
4.			
5.			
6.			
7.			
8.			
9.			
10.			
11.			
12.			

Total $_______

Outline Your Experiment

This sheet is designed to help you outline your experiment. If you need more space, make a copy of this page to finish your outline. When you are done with this sheet, review it with an adult, make any necessary changes, review safety concerns on the next page, prepare your data tables, gather your equipment, and start to experiment.

In the space below, list what you are going to do in the order you are going to do it.

i. ______________________________

____

____

____

ii. ______________________________

____

____

____

iii. ______________________________

____

____

____

iv. ______________________________

____

____

____

v. ______________________________

____

____

____

Evaluate Safety Concerns

We have included an overall safety section in the front of this book on pages 16–18, but there are some very specific questions you need to ask, and prepare for, depending on the needs of your experiment. If you find that you need to prepare for any of these safety concerns, place a check mark next to the letter.

____ *A. Goggles & Eyewash Station*

If you are mixing chemicals or working with materials that might splinter or produce flying objects, goggles and an eyewash station or sink with running water should be available.

____ *B. Ventilation*

If you are mixing chemicals that could produce fire, smoke, fumes, or obnoxious odors, you will need to use a vented hood or go outside and perform the experiment in the fresh air.

____ *C. Fire Blanket or Fire Extinguisher*

If you are working with potentially combustible chemicals or electricity, a fire blanket and extinguisher nearby are a must.

____ *D. Chemical Disposal*

If your experiment produces a poisonous chemical or there are chemical-filled tissues (as in dissected animals), you may need to make arrangements to dispose of the by-products from your lab.

____ *E. Electricity*

If you are working with materials and developing an idea that uses electricity, make sure that the wires are in good repair, that the electrical demand does not exceed the capacity of the supply, and that your work area is grounded.

____ *F. Emergency Phone Numbers*

Look up and record the following phone numbers for the Fire Department: ______________ , Poison Control: ______________ , and Hospital: ______________. Post them in an easy-to-find location.

Prepare Data Tables

Finally, you will want to prepare your data tables and have them ready to go before you start your experiment. Each data table should be easy to understand and easy for you to use.

A good data table has a **title** that describes the information being collected, and it identifies the **variable** and the **unit** being collected on each data line. The variable is *what* you are measuring and the unit is *how* you are measuring it. They are usually written like this:

Variable (unit), or to give you some examples:

Time (seconds)
Distance (meters)
Electricity (volts)

An example of a well-prepared data table looks like the sample below. We've cut the data table into thirds because the book is too small to display the whole line.

Determining the Boiling Point of Compound X_1

Time (min.)	0	1	2	3	4	5	6
Temp. (°C)							

Time (min.)	7	8	9	10	11	12	13
Temp. (°C)							

Time (min.)	14	15	16	17	18	19	20
Temp. (°C)							

Scientific Method
• Step 4 •
Conduct the Experiment

Lab Time

It's time to get going. You've generated a hypothesis, collected the materials, written out the procedure, checked the safety issues, and prepared your data tables. Fire it up. Here's the short list of things to remember as you experiment.

____ *A. Follow the Procedure, Record Any Changes*

Follow your own directions specifically as you wrote them. If you find the need to change the procedure once you are into the experiment, that's fine; it's part of the process. Make sure to keep detailed records of the changes. When you repeat the experiment a second or third time, follow the new directions exactly.

____ *B. Observe Safety Rules*

It's easier to complete the lab activity if you are in the lab rather than the emergency room.

____ *C. Record Data Immediately*

Collect temperatures, distances, voltages, revolutions, and any other variables and immediately record them into your data table. Do not think you will be able to remember them and fill everything in after the lab is completed.

____ *D. Repeat the Experiment Several Times*

The more data that you collect, the better. It will give you a larger data base and your averages are more meaningful. As you do multiple experiments, be sure to identify each data set by date and time so you can separate them out.

____ *E. Prepare for Extended Experiments*

Some experiments require days or weeks to complete, particularly those with plants and animals or the growing of crystals. Prepare a safe place for your materials so your experiment can continue undisturbed while you collect the data. Be sure you've allowed enough time for your due date.

Scientific Method
• Step 5 •
Collect and Display Data

Types of Graphs

This section will give you some ideas on how you can display the information you are going to collect as a graph. A graph is simply a picture of the data that you gathered portrayed in a manner that is quick and easy to reference. There are four kinds of graphs described on the next two pages. If you find you need a leg up in the graphing department, we have a book in the series called *Data Tables & Graphing*. It will guide you through the process.

Line and Bar Graphs

These are the most common kinds of graphs. The most consistent variable is plotted on the "x", or horizontal, axis and the more temperamental variable is plotted along the "y", or vertical, axis. Each data point on a line graph is recorded as a dot on the graph and then all of the dots are connected to form a picture of the data. A bar graph starts on the horizontal axis and moves up to the data line.

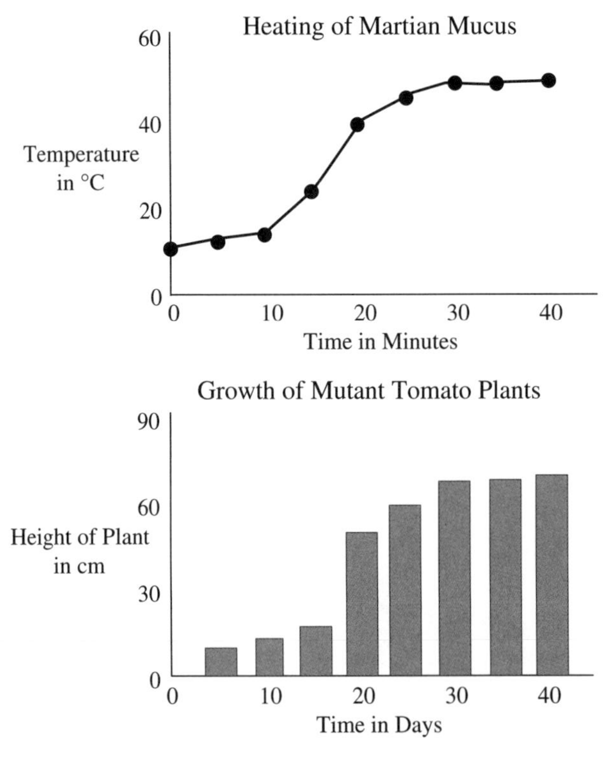

Best Fit Graphs

A best fit graph was created to show averages or trends rather than specific data points. The data that has been collected is plotted on a graph just as on a line graph, but instead of drawing a line from point to point to point, which sometimes is impossible anyway, you just free hand a line that hits "most of the data."

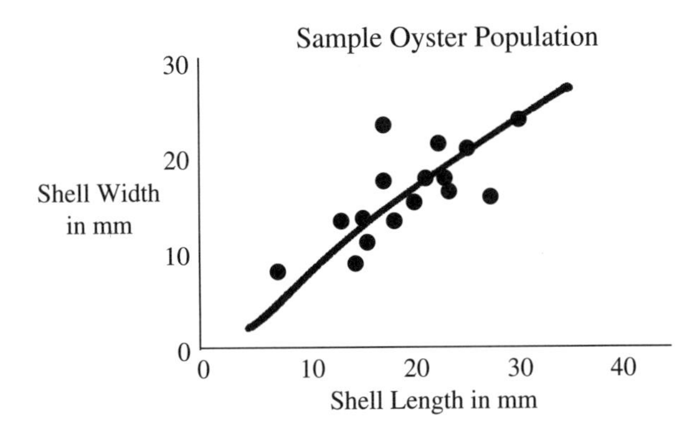

Pie Graphs

Pie graphs are used to show relationships between different groups. All of the data is totaled up and a percentage is determined for each group. The pie is then divided to show the relationship of one group to another.

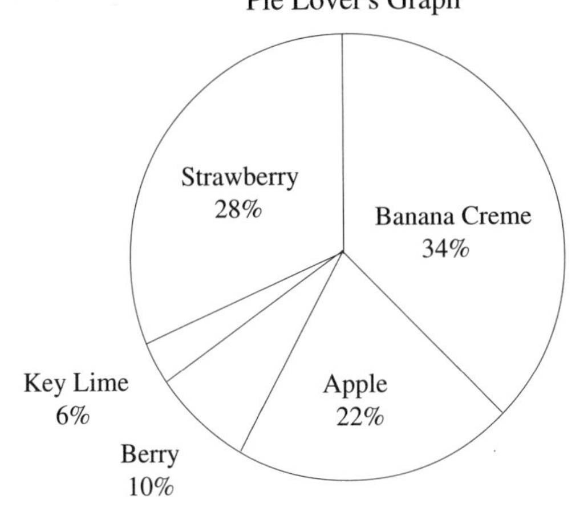

Other Kinds of Data

1. Written Notes & Observations

This is the age-old technique used by all scientists. Record your observations in a lab book. Written notes can be made quickly as the experiment is proceeding, and they can then be expounded upon later. Quite often notes made in the heat of an experiment are revisited during the evaluation portion of the process, and they can shed valuable light on how or why the experiment went the way it did.

2. Drawings

Quick sketches as well as fully developed drawings can be used as a way to report data for a science experiment. Be sure to title each drawing and, if possible, label what it is that you are looking at. Drawings that are actual size are best.

3. Photographs, Videotapes, and Audiotapes

Usually better than drawings, quicker, and more accurate, but you do have the added expense and time of developing the film. However, they can often capture images and details that are not usually seen by the naked eye.

4. The Experiment Itself

Some of the best data you can collect and present is the actual experiment itself. Nothing will speak more effectively for you than the plants you grew, the specimens you collected, or that big pile of tissue that was an armadillo you peeled from the tread of an 18-wheeler.

Scientific Method
• Step 6 •
Present Your Ideas

Oral Report Checklist

It is entirely possible that you will be asked to make an oral presentation to your classmates. This will give you an opportunity to explain what you did and how you did it. Quite often this presentation is part of your overall score, so if you do well, it will enhance your chances for one of the bigger awards.

To prepare for your oral report, your science fair presentation should include the following components:

Physical Display

_____a. freestanding display board
- hypothesis
- data tables, graphs, photos, etc.
- abstract (short summary)

_____b. actual lab setup (equipment)

Oral Report

_____a. hypothesis or question

_____b. background information
- concepts
- word definitions
- history or scientists

_____c. experimental procedure

_____d. data collected
- data tables
- graphs
- photos or drawings

_____e. conclusions and findings

_____f. ask for questions

Set the display board up next to you on the table. Transfer the essential information to index cards. Use the index cards for reference, but do not read from them. Speak in a clear voice, hold your head up, and make eye contact with your peers. Ask if there are any questions before you finish and sit down.

Written Report Checklist

Next up is the written report, also called your lab write-up. After you compile or sort the data you have collected during the experiment and evaluate the results, you will be able to come to a conclusion about your hypothesis. Remember, disproving an idea is as valuable as proving it.

This sheet is designed to help you write up your science fair project and present your data in an organized manner. This is a final checklist for you.

To prepare your write-up, your science fair report should include the following components:

_____ a. binder
_____ b. cover page, title, & your name
_____ c. abstract (one paragraph summary)
_____ d. table of contents with page numbers
_____ e. hypothesis or question
_____ f. background information
    concepts
    word definitions
    history or scientists
_____ g. list of materials used
_____ h. experimental procedure
    written description
    photo or drawing of setup
_____ i. data collected
    data tables
    graphs
    photos or drawings
_____ j. conclusions and findings
_____ k. glossary of terms
_____ l. references

Display Checklist

2. Prepare your display to accompany the report. A good display should include the following:

Freestanding Display

_____ a. freestanding cardboard back
_____ b. title of experiment
_____ c. your name
_____ d. hypothesis
_____ e. findings of the experiment
_____ f. photo or illustrations of equipment
_____ g. data tables or graphs

Additional Display Items

_____ h. a copy of the write-up
_____ i. actual lab equipment setup

Glossary, Index, and More Ideas

Glossary

Acids

Any compound that has a pH below 7.0. These materials have lots of free hydrogen atoms to react with other compounds. Some common examples of acids are found in oranges, grapefruits, lemons, tangerines, and strawberries.

Atom

The smallest complete building block of the universe. These are also elements and as of this writing there were just over 100 of them. Some of the more famous are oxygen, carbon, hydrogen, gold, lead, copper, helium, iron, calcium, and einsteinium.

Bipolar Molecule

A molecule with a strange mental disorder . . . nope, check that. A fixed arrangement of atoms. If one end of the molecule exhibits a positive charge and the other end exhibits a negative charge, it is said to be bipolar or have two poles. They are like little magnets and are very important in transferring other atoms through wall membranes, cell walls, and other biochemical check points.

Boiling Point

The temperature that a compound changes from a liquid to a gas. Fixed for each and every compound, this is an identifying trait that allows chemists to identify and separate compounds.

Buoyant Force

The upward pressure exerted by a liquid on an object floating in that liquid—a function, in part, of the density of that liquid.

Change of State

The term, "state" refers to solids, liquids, and gases. When a liquid changes from a solid to a liquid or liquid to a solid, when a liquid changes to a gas or a gas to a liquid, or if a solid changes to a gas, it is called a change of state. No relocation necessary.

Glossary

Chemical Change

Two or more chemicals combining to form a new compound with new characteristics. Indicators of this are a change in state, color, temperature, density, odor, or magnetism. This new compound also has a new boiling point, melting point, density, and so on. It's a complete makeover from a molecular point of view.

Chemical Formulas

A combination of letters and numbers representing molecules and atoms. Written as an equation showing the changes and new by-products. Shorthand for chemists.

Chromotography

The separation of colors, pigments, or molecules in general, by using a solvent and a porous piece of paper or a gel and an electrical charge. The compound separate from lightest to heaviest or by charges.

Cohesion

Attraction between two bipolar molecules. Generally not something that we discuss in front of the kids.

Colloid

A solid, liquid, or gas dispersed into a second solid, liquid, or gas but not chemically connected to that other compound. Styrofoam is one of the more famous examples. Air is trapped in spaces created when polystyrene plastic is extracted from a mold. The air is still air, the polystyrene is still polystyrene. They just happen to like to hang out together.

Convection Current

The movement of hot air or water in an upward motion relative to the cooler surrounding air or liquid. Warm liquids or gases rise and cool ones sink. This sinking and rising create a current.

Glossary

Crystallization

The slow cooling or evaporation of a liquid that allows for the orderly deposition of atoms and molecules to form solid crystals. The slower the process the bigger the crystals.

Density

Mass divided by volume. The number tells you how tightly packed the atoms in your sample are compared with other samples.

Effervescence

Gas displaced in a liquid by a solid. When this happens, the gas can leave in a big hurry and produce a tremendous amount of foam.

Elements

Atoms. The Periodic Table of the Elements is the Yellow Pages™ of the atom community and provides information about structure, reactivity, state, and mass among other things.

Emulsion

Two liquids that have been mixed together and remain mixed but do not react with one another chemically. Mayonnaise is an excellent example of egg yolks and oil.They have been beaten together but have not reacted with one another to form a brand new compound.

Endothermic

A chemical reaction that absorbs heat from the environment. It feels cool to the touch.

Evaporation

A change in state from liquid to gas.

Exothermic

A chemical reaction that releases heat in to the environment. It feels warm or hot to the touch.

Glossary

Filtering

A method of separating mixtures by pouring them through a porous piece of paper called a filter. Once in the paper, the liquids pass through and the solids remain on the surface. Coffee anyone?

Freezing Point

The temperature at which a free-flowing liquid changes to a solid compound. For deer, it is the minute that the car turns the bend and the headlights illuminate them. Fixed for each and every compound, this is an identifying trait that allows chemists to identify and separate compounds. Cousin to the melting point.

Graphs

Quick, easy-to-view pictures of data. There are several kinds of graphs: pie, bar, line, best fit, and pictorial.

Hydrophilic

A molecule or compound that is absorbed by or is solvent in water. *Water-loving* is the literal translation from the Latin.

Hydrophobic

A molecule or compound that is repelled by water. *Water-fearing* is the literal translation from the Latin.

Insolubility

A compound, solid, liquid, or gas that will not dissolve into another liquid or gas—they do not play well with one another.

Melting Point

A fixed, characteristic temperature where a compound changes from a solid to a liquid. Fixed for each and every compound, this is an identifying trait that allows chemists to identify and separate compounds. Cousin to the freezing point.

Meniscus

A dip or downward bow in the level of the water held in a narrow cylinder. The bottom level of the meniscus is an accurate reflection of the amount of water in the container.

Physical Change

Tearing, ripping, folding, stomping, squashing, or any other random mutilation exacted on a compound that does not change its chemical nature or inherent characteristics.

Solvent

A liquid or gas that allows a second, different compound to disperse or dissolve in between its molecules.

Sublimation

A relatively unusual compound that changes directly from a gas to a solid or a solid to gas without taking time to pass through the liquid state. Dry ice is a great example of this.

Suspension

Solid particles evenly mixed into and floating around in a liquid. Milk is a suspension of protein and fat in liquid.

Thermometer

A tool that measures the average amount of heat in a substance.

Whey

Response to the statement, "No Whey!" Apologies to Wayne and Garth, we succumbed to the temptation to entertain a very thin portion of the demographic.

Whey is actually the heavier liquid layer that is leftover when a dilute acid is added to milk, and the fat and protein curdle and float on top of the liquid. Sorry, the opportunity for a joke was too much to pass up. End of glossary, hope you had fun.

Index

Acids
- Acetic, 104
- Muriatic (hydrochloric), 62
- Sulfuric, 90–91

Air, 22, 24
Atom, 79

Bipolar molecule, 156
Boiling point, 68, 129
Borax, 125
Building a Research Foundation, 205–207
Buoyant force, 39, 40

Change of state, 100
Chemical
- Formulas, 97–98
- Reactions, 102

Chemical change, 100, 104, 111, 112, 113
Chromatography, 139, 141
Cohesion, 26
Colloid, 124, 125, 183
Color, 90, 104, 111
Condensation points, 64
Convection current, 148
Crystallization, 129
Curds, 124

Data
- Other kinds of, 218
- Prepare tables for, 212

Density, 32, 35, 37, 41
Dinosaurs, 189
Display checklist, 222
Dry ice, 36, 42, 43, 184

Index

Effervescence, 28
Electrostatic effect, 161
Elements, 80–83
Periodic Table of, 80, 134
Emulsion, 119, 121
Endothermic, 76
Evaporation, 107, 135, 138
Exothermic, 76

Filtering, 129, 130
Flexibility, 49
Freezing point, 64, 129

Gather information, 204–207
Glossary 224–227
Graphs
Bar, 216
Best Fit, 217
Line, 216
Pie, 217
Types of, 216–217

Heat loss, 49
How tadpoles change into frogs, 190
Hydrophilic, 174, 182
Hydrophobic, 174
Hypothesis, 195, 202

Insolubility, 134

Kelvin scale, 49

Lab materials
Acquire your, 209

Index

Magnetism, 84, 85, 134
Measurement
    English system, 50, 52, 53
    Metric system, 50, 52, 53
    Medieval Europe, 50, 51, 52
Melting point, 64, 69
Meniscus, 55, 158–159
Moose, Majestic The, 190

Odor, 86, 129
Oral Report Checklist, 220

Original
    Experiment, 187
    Idea, 187
    Question, 187

pH, 149–151
Physical change, 111, 112, 113, 114
Polar molecule, 169, 171
Potential energy, 165
Precipitation, 129, 131, 133

Safety, 16–18
    Evaluate concerns and, 211
Shape, 88–89
Solubility, 134
Solvent, 117
Sublimation, 42, 69, 136, 185
Surface tension, 167, 169, 170, 171, 173
Suspension, 123
Thermometer, defined, 46

Vaporization, 64
Written Report Checklist, 221

More Science Books

Catch a Wave
40 hands-on lab activities that sound off on the topic of noise, vibration, waves, the Doppler Effect and associated ideas.

Thermodynamic Thrills
35 hands-on lab activities that investigate heat via conduction, convection, radiation, specific heat, and temperature.

Relatively Albert
50 hands-on lab activities that explore the world of mechanics, forces, gravity, and Newton's three laws of motion.

Gravity Works
50 hands-on lab activities from the world of things that fly. Air, air pressure, Bernoulli's law, and all things that fly, float, or glide are explored.

Electron Herding 101
50 hands-on lab activities that introduce static electricity, circuit electricity, and include a number of fun, and very easy-to-build projects.

Opposites Attract
50 hands-on lab activities that delve into the world of natural and man-made magnets as well as the characteristics of magnetic attraction.